Mahabaleshwar

Mahabaleshwar

RAO BAHADUR D. B. PARASNIS

GYAN

Published by

Gyan Publishing House
5, Ansari Road
Daryaganj, New Delhi-110002
Phone: 011-47034999, 9811692060
E-mail: books@gyanbooks.com

Distribution Network
gyanbooks.com
India, USA, Canada, UK, Australia, France

ISBN : 978-81-212-9530-7 (PB)
First Published, 1916

2nd Impression 2023

Printed at: Gyan Press, Delhi.

Mahabaleshwar
Author: RAO BAHADUR D. B. PARASNIS

Mahabaleshwar.

H. E. LORD WILLINGDON.

H. E. LADY WILLINGDON.

Mahabaleshwar.

"Over the wild mountains and luxuriant plains
Nature in all the pomp of beauty reigns."

—*James Montgomery.*

BY

RAO BAHADUR D. B. PARASNIS,
HAPPY VALE, SATARA.

1916.

To

THEIR EXCELLENCIES

The Right Hon'ble LORD WILLINGDON, G.C.I.E.,

GOVERNOR OF BOMBAY,

AND

LADY WILLINGDON,

THIS BOOK

IS

WITH THEIR GRACIOUS PERMISSION

DEDICATED.

PREFACE.

At the desire of many interested friends, I have endeavoured to put together in this book all available information about the charming hills of Mahabaleshwar, and it is hoped that it will be found equally interesting and useful by all those who visit this place and wish to know something of its history and climate.

I beg to offer my respectful thanks to the Government of Bombay for their kind permission to me to see the old Residency Records of Satara, from which I obtained much valuable information on the subject. I have also to acknowledge my indebtedness to several eminent authorities on Mahabaleshwar, such as Dr. James Murray, Sir George Birdwood and others, from whose rare and valuable works I derived considerable help; and to many of my personal friends from whom I received advice and assistance in various ways.

D. B. P.

CONTENTS.

APPENDICES.

LIST OF ILLUSTRATIONS.

MAHABALESHWAR.

CHAPTER I.

EARLY HISTORY.

THE most delightful and picturesque hills of Mahabaleshwar are situated in 17° 51′ N. L. and 73° 30′ E. L. in the Jaoli Taluka of the Satara District, and are about thirty miles north-west of Satara and twenty miles west of Wai. They form one of the spurs of the great Sahyadri range, which is well-known as the Western Ghauts. These rolling spurs, crowned by flat-topped summits, command magnificent views of deep valleys, and possess natural advantages surpassed by few. The principal Sanatorium of the Bombay Presidency is established on the summits of these hills, with a general elevation of 4,500 feet above sea-level, rising at its highest point, the Sindola Hill, to 4,700 feet. It is reached from Bombay by the Great Indian Peninsula Railway to Poona, and thence by the Madras and S. M. Railway to Wathar Station, from which it is 40 miles distant. Formerly, the traveller from Bombay used to go by sea to Dasgaon and Mahad, near the mouth of the river Savitri, and proceed to Mahabaleshwar by a fine road, leading across the hilly country, interspersed with woody dales and level planes of luxuriant cultivation. These hills, aptly termed as 'Mild Paradise of Beauty,' with their fine climate and sublime features, enjoy the highest popularity, and have become the favourite summer retreat of the Government of Bombay.

The name Mahabaleshwar, given to these hills, is full of meaning, which indicates the greatness of this place. The word 'Maha-bala-Ishwar' is made up of three Sanskrit words, namely, महा, बल and ईश्वर, which put together mean 'the God of Great Power.' Thus the name of the powerful God Mahadev, given to these hills, suggests the idea of sanctity and holiness, which is generally attributed to lofty mountains and high places. It is remarkable that such a belief is prevalent not only in India, but in almost all the countries of the world from ancient times. The reason is apparent. The elevated position, the silence, and the tranquility of hills and mountains naturally aid contemplation, awaken spiritual thought and inspire devotion to God. The term 'High Places,' frequently mentioned in the Holy Scriptures, has its origin in the most ancient practice of performing religious worship on the tops of mountains. In Eastern countries high mountains have been held in great reverence. The Chinese entertain a belief that Heaven made the lofty hills for the abode of gods and spirits. In India, the Hindus regard with great veneration all the important mountains and hills; and the sources of rivers, which flow from them, are held in great sanctity. They are dedicated to some god who is worshipped with great religious devotion. The snow-clad pinnacles of the great Himalayas possess the sacred Gangotri—the source of the great river Ganges. At the eastern apex of the Satpura range, from the holy summit of Amarkantak issues forth the river Narmada, the banks of which are adorned with many temples and ghats. From another plateau of Satpura rises the river Tapti from the sacred tank of Multapi, which is supposed to possess purifying virtues. The Godavari, which is only surpassed by the Ganges in sanctity and picturesque scenery, rises from the high and precipitous mountain of Trimbakeshwar (the three-eyed God Mahadev), which is a sacred spot in the Nasik District; and the river Bhima rises from the well-known shrine of Bhima-Shankar (another name of Mahadev) on the crest of the Western Ghauts, which possesses one of the twelve *Lingams* of Shiva, known as *Jotirlingams*. From these instances it will appear that the most remarkable hills in the country are rendered more or less sacred by the establishment of shrines or places of worship, dedicated to some god at the source of a river. The river Krishna being one of the famous rivers of the Deccan, great sanctity is attached to its source at Mahabaleshwar; and in a legendary account, called the *Krishnâ Mâhâtmya*, the importance of the river is fully described. There is also another work, called the *Mahabaleshwar Puran*, which contains only a short description of the village and the sacred pools and temples, as now shown by the priests. Both the tracts are, however, modern compositions and possess little value from an historical point of view.*

The early history of Mahabaleshwar is shrouded in obscurity. The first mention, that is found in old papers, is of the

* These tracts were brought to the notice of the public by the late Rao Saheb V. N. Mandlik in the two interesting papers, read by him before the Bombay Branch of the Royal Asiatic Society, in 1870-71.

visit to Mahabaleshwar of the famous Yadav king, Singhan (A.D. 1210–1247), in the early part of the thirteenth century. It is well-known that the Yadav kings of Devgiri were very powerful rulers and their rule extended all over Maharashtra. Singhan was well-known for his bravery and led his conquests upto Gujarath and Malwa. He subdued Bhoj II, the king of Panhala, and annexed the Kolhapur kingdom of the Shilahar dynasty to his dominions about A.D. 1211. On account of his glorious victories, honourific titles signifying paramount sovereignty, such as *Akhil-jagadadhar* (the support of the whole world) *Prithvi-wallabha* (the lover of the earth) *Rajadhiraj* (king of kings) were given to him in old inscriptions, from which it appears that the empire of the Yadav kings of Devgiri was at its zenith during his reign, and a large portion of the Deccan was included in it. This king was a great patron of learning and arts; and the famous treatise on music, *Sangit-Ratnakar*, by Sharangadhar, was composed in his time. It is this illustrious prince, who first paid a visit to Mahabaleshwar and built a small tank at the source of the Krishna, as well as a temple of the God Mahabaleshwar about the year A.D. 1215. He presented dresses, ornaments and several other articles to the God, and appointed one Babaji Koli as manager of the temple. The name of Singhan is still cherished at Mahabaleshwar, and the place where he bathed in the holy waters of the Krishna is known as *Singhan Doha*, near Nandagane, a village in the Krishna valley, close to Mahabaleshwar. There is another place, called Singnapur in the Man Taluka of the Satara District, which is also named after this great king. From these facts it appears that the Yadav kings were in possession of the country round Miraj and Panhala, and the hilly parts of the Deccan, including Mahabaleshwar, remained for some time under their nominal control.

The Mabableshwar hills and the country surrounding them were virtually held by the Shirkes in the thirteenth century; but it is not known whether they were independent or owed allegiance to the Yadav kings. Captain Grant Duff only mentions:— "The Shirkes obtained possession of the country about the source of the Krishna after the Raja of Panhala was conquered in the beginning of the thirteenth century by the Raja Singhan." This Maratha family of the Shirkes was highly respected in Maharashtra for its ancient descent and is conspicuous in the history of the Marathas. Its founder, Vangoji, or Vajrapal, conquered 84 villages in the Tal Konkan, probably in the thirteenth century, which is still known as *Shirkan Tappa* (the country of the Shirkes). His descendants, who were styled polygars or independent kings of the Konkan, held the country under their sway for many generations. On the overthrow of the Yadav dynasty of Devgiri by the Mahomedans in 1318, the governors appointed by the Emperors of Delhi ruled over Maharashtra; but owing to their oppressive and unjust rule, there was wide-spread disorder which led to the successful revolt of the Deccan nobles under their able leader, Ala-ud-din Hasan Gangu, who freed the Deccan from the control of the Emperors of Delhi in 1347. Hasan Gangu founded a new dynasty, called Brahmani or Bahmani, in honour of his Brahmin patron Gangadhar Pant, and fixed his capital at Gulburga, which was removed to Bedar in 1429. Under the rule of the Bahmani dynasty, the country enjoyed peace and prosperity for some time. But it experienced the dreadful calamity of the Durgadevi famine from 1396 to 1407, which left the country in total desolation. The Shirkes, who were at this time very powerful in the Konkan, took this opportunity to extend their possessions and to capture strong places from the Bahmani government. In 1453 Malik-ul-Tujar was sent from Bedar to reduce the independent local chiefs like the Shirkes and to recover the lost territory; but the most subtle and daring chief of the Shirke family, who then held the Konkan independently, assuming an air of great humility, decoyed the Bahmani governor and killed him while marching against the Hindu Prince Shankar Ray of Khelna (Vishalgad). The name of this Shirke chief is supposed to be Vangoji II, who held possession of all the Konkan Ghat-matha from Poona to the river Warna—"a mountainous tract, in which," says Captain Clunes, "were preserved those seeds of Hindu independence, which at no very distant period, sprang up a goodly tree extending its branches to the remotest corners of India."*

The Shirkes lived for some time in the fort of Bahiravgad and then made Rairi (afterwards Raygad) their capital. At the end of the fifteenth century, the Bahmani empire was divided into five small kingdoms, of which Bijapur and Ahmednagar ruled over the Deccan for nearly two

* The Native Princes of India by Captain Clunes.

hundred years. By that time the Shirkes lost their independence and became their vassals. The sympathetic rule and religious toleration of the Musulman kings of Bijapur and Ahmednagar attracted the Hindu nobles and chieftains to their courts. Many of them were employed in high posts in the military and civil departments, and were rewarded with high titles and jahagirs for their loyal and distinguished services. The Shirkes of Rairi, Raja Waghoji and his son, Raja Tanhoji, joined the Nizamshahi kings of Ahmednagar, and were granted Sardeshmukhi of 12 Mahals with Rairi or Raygad as their capital, retaining the possession of the sacred hills of Mahabaleshwar. They usually resided at Ahmednagar and appointed one Dalpat Rao as their representative to manage their affairs at Rairi, who preserved peace and order in the country.

The Shirkes exercised great influence over the Nizamshahi kings of Ahmednagar and enjoyed their favour and confidence. They took active part in the quarrels between the Ahmednagar and Bijapur governments and gave much trouble to the latter in the middle of the sixteenth century, which led to the suppression of their power and made way for another Maratha family, surnamed More, who flourished under the Bijapur kings and became the rulers of Jaoli and Mahabaleshwar. The Shirkes, after their defeat by Chandra Rao More, took shelter at Shringarpur in the Konkan with the Surve Rajas of that place. They were for a time crest-fallen, but regained their influence in the reign of Shivaji, who highly valued their help and entered into relationship with their family. Their descendants, who enjoyed the Deshmukhi vatan of Dabhol, afterwards dwindled to the rank of respectable Silledars in the Maratha kingdom.

The founder of the More family is believed to be Parsoji Bajirao More, who flourished in the beginning of the sixteenth century. He was an officer in the Carnatic army and was appointed in the reign of Usuf Adil Shah (1490–1510) to the command of 12,000 Hindu infantry, and was asked to subdue the tract between the Nira and the Warna rivers in the Deccan, then held by the Shirkes. In this enterprise More was successful. He reduced to submission the discendants of Shirkes and their partisans, named Gujars, Mamulkars, Mohites, and Mahadiks. For these valuable services he was rewarded with the title of Chandra Rao and granted the jahagir of Jaoli containing 18 mahals, including Ategaon and Murhe in the Tal Konkan. His son, Yeshwant Rao, distinguished himself in the battle of Parenda with the army of Burhan Nizam Shah (1508-1553), and captured the enemy's green flag as a trophy. For his bravery he was confirmed in the succession to his father as the Raja of Jaoli, and permitted to use the standard he had won. The exact date of More's succession to the kingdom of Jaoli cannot be ascertained owing to want of authentic evidence. But it may be safely assumed that the Mores were in possession of Jaoli and Mahabaleshwar in the latter part of the sixteenth century. "Their posterity," writes Grant Duff, "ruled in the same tract of country for seven generations; and by their wise and useful administration, that inhospitable region became extremely populous. All the successors of the first More assumed the title of Chandra Rao. The invariable submission manifested by this Raja probably induced the government to exact little more than a nominal tribute from districts producing so little, and which had always been in disorder under Mahomedan management."

In the absence of authentic information, it is not possible to trace correctly the seven generations of the Mores, who ruled over Jaoli and Mahabaleshwar. It may, however, be observed that the Raja of Jaoli, who made considerable efforts to improve the sacred place of Mahabaleshwar, was Krishnaji Baji Chandra Rao More. He had taken a vow before the God Mahabaleshwar, that he would offer a silver image of half a maund, if he would be successful in quelling the disturbances of the Kolis in the Deccan, who had become very troublesome in those days. By the blessings of the God Mahabaleshwar, he gained complete success, and accordingly he presented to the shrine the silver article in 1578. Raja Chandra Rao was a very liberal and charitably disposed person, who was a great devotee of the God Mahabaleshwar. He newly built the temple of Mahabaleshwar and also that of the five rivers at great cost. He presented many valuable articles to these temples. On account of his religious devotion and charitable deeds, he was styled 'Dharmraja' (the name of the eldest brother of the Pandavas, who was known for his generosity, charity and truthfulness). He had five sons, namely:—Balaji Rao, Daulat Rao, Hanmant Rao, Govind Rao and Yeshwant Rao, amongst whom he divided his jahagir.

RAJA SHIVAJI.

(A. D. 1627–A. D. 1680).

He gave the village of Jaoli to Balaji Rao Shivthar to Daulat Rao, Jor to Hanmant Rao, Jambli to Govind Rao, and Bahuli to Yeshwant Rao. The hereditary titles of 'Raja' and 'Chandra Rao,' and all the emblems of authority were given to Balaji Rao as he was the eldest son. All these brothers were great devotees of the God Mahabaleshwar to whom they made munificent gifts of land and money.

While the Rajas of Jaoli established their power in the country south of Poona, stretching from the Ghauts to the upper Krishna, and attained great importance in the Bijapur court, the beginning of the seventeenth century witnessed a great political event. A great Maratha hero appeared in the Deccan and attempted successfully to establish an independent Hindu kingdom. It was Shivaji, the founder of the Maratha empire and champion of the Hindu faith, who was born at Shivneri near Junnar in 1627. His father, Shahaji, son of Maloji Bhonsle, was a great military leader in the Mahomedan kingdoms of Ahmednagar and Bijapur, whose rulers were tolerant towards the Hindus and utilised their services alike in warfare and civil administration. Maloji Bhonsle rose to great distinction in the service of Nizam Shah of Ahmednagar, and held the command of 5,000 horse with the title of Raja, and got a jahagir for the maintenance of his dignity and force. He acquitted himself well in the several offices he had been appointed to and died in 1619. His son, Shahaji, succeeded to his jahagir, which consisted chiefly of Poona, Supa and Chakan districts. During the continuance of wars in the Deccan between the Imperial armies of the Mogals and those of Ahmednagar and Bijapur, Shahaji was engaged successively on behalf of the Deccan kingdoms, still retaining his jahagir. On the conquest of Ahmednagar in 1636, Shahaji transferred his allegiance to the king of Bijapur, who bestowed on him a command (*Mansub*) and a jahagir. He was subsequently employed by the Bijapur government to subdue the countries in the South, and obtained larger jahagirs in Mysore, including the forts of Sira and Bangalore, where he made his head-quarters and lived till his death in 1664.

Shivaji spent his boyhood at Poona with his mother. His education and the management of the jahagir estate were entrusted by Shahaji to one Dadoji Kondev, a loyal and faithful Brahmin servant. Shivaji's extraordinary talents and his natural love for his country and religion were soon developed in the congenial atmosphere of the Deccan; they created in him an inspiration to free his country from the tyrany and oppression of the Mahomedan rulers of those days. "The central authority at Bijapur," writes Prof. Owen, was weak, distracted by internal dissensions during a minority, and by the threatening attitude and aggressive movements of Shah Jehan's representative, Prince Aurangzeb. The young Shivaji saw his opportunity, and several years before the Prince became the Emperor, entered on an ingenious, daring and systematic course of self-aggrandisement and ambition. But never was a great revolution begun more quietly and unostentatiously. A movement which was to pervade and convulse all India took its rise, like one of the Deccan rivers, in a corner and in the bosom of the hills."*

The account of the wonderful rise of this great hero is fully described by Grant Duff in his History of the Marathas. It will suffice to say here that Shivaji, imbued with lofty notions of Hindu nationality, cherished from his boyhood

* The Fall of the Mogul Empire by Prof. Sidney J. Owen, pp. 56-57.

the ambition of founding a Hindu kingdom. He collected around him hardy and active hillmen from the Ghauts, known as Mawlis, seized fort after fort, and was soon able to establish himself in the tract between Chakan and the Nira. The astonishing rapidity, with which he made these acquisitions, called forth no opposition on the part of the king of Bijapur for some time. But the capture of the forts of Torna and Rajgad by Shivaji in 1648, soon attracted notice and awakened the court of Bijapur to his real designs. The king of Bijapur naturally suspected that Shivaji's activities were connived at by Shahaji; he therefore first endeavoured to strike at the root by putting Shahaji into prison to bring pressure on Shivaji. But Shivaji with his superior wisdom and sagacity made friendly peace with Shaha Jehan, Emperor of Delhi; and through his intercession, secured the release of his father. The hostilities between Shivaji and the Bijapur king were continued successively for ten years, and the latter made great efforts to surprise and capture him. Orders were issued to Jahagirdars and Deshmukhs to seize Shivaji and to suppress his revolt. Expeditions were sent against him under distinguished military commanders to crush his power. But Shivaji had by that time become so powerful and formidable by repairing and guarding his newly conquered hill-forts, collecting a brave army of devoted Mawlis, and inviting the patriotic Marathas to his standard, that he soon began to measure his strength against Bijapur and to dictate his own terms.

The struggle between Shivaji and Bijapur brought him into close contact with the Maratha jahagirdars, such as Ghorpades, Mores, Sawants, Dalwis, Manes, Nimbalkars and Ghatges, who enjoyed handsome jahagirs and high positions under the Mahomedan rule of Bijapur, and who were loyally attached to it. Shivaji, with the noble object of national emancipation, desired to secure their co-operation and help. But these feudal chiefs did not first realise the importance of his mission and looked upon him as a rebel. Not only did they not join him, but they actually worked to undermine his influence and put down his power. Shivaji had, therefore, to get rid of these opponents and smoothen his way to the realization of his object. The first Maratha jahagirdar, dealt with by him, was Chandra Rao More, the Raja of Jaoli, who held at the time an extensive territory including the sacred hills of Mahabaleshwar.

As mentioned above, the Mores of Jaoli held the Ghautmatha of Sahyadri as part of their jahagir, which had great strategical advantages on account of its strong hill-forts and difficult passes. Raja Balaji Chandra Rao was an influential and powerful jahagirdar of the Bijapur kingdom, having an army 10,000 strong in his service. Shivaji first made efforts to induce Chandra Rao to join him in his national undertaking, but he declined. From an old sanad issued to a learned Brahmin of Mahabaleshwar, Gopal Bhat bin Shridhar Bhat, it appears that Shivaji and his mother Jijabai visited the sacred place of Mahabaleshwar in 1653 and took spiritual advice from him. At this time the country was under the rule of Chandra Rao More; and it was probable that Shivaji might have gained correct information of the situation and strength of the principal places in the vicinity. Chandra Rao had three beautiful daughters; and it was the desire of Shivaji's mother to unite the two families by a blood relationship and cement the union for a noble purpose. But Chandra Rao More did not like the idea, as he thought his dignity, rank and status far superior to those of Shivaji. Chandra Rao vainly boasted of the titles and honours, conferred on his family by the kings of Bijapur, while he considered that Shivaji's claim was never recognised by any paramount power. Although Chandra Rao received all the messengers of Shivaji with every courtesy, he refused to join him in his hostilities against the Bijapur government. On the contrary, he gave protection and assistance to the Bijapur army under Baji Shamraj, who was sent to surprise and capture Shivaji. This afforded sufficient excuse for Shivaji to act in open hostility against Chandra Rao More.

Chandra Rao, who was said to be addicted to intoxicating drugs and other vices, became most unpopular with his brothers and relations. Some of them being dissatisfied with him actually joined Shivaji, who promised them help and support. Chandra Rao carried on a secret correspondence against Shivaji with the Bijapur government and formed secret plans against him. On one occasion, it is mentioned in 'the Mahabaleshwar Account,' that he engaged even the Guravs, worshippers of the Mahabaleshwar temple, in his secret machinations with Bijapur. Shivaji therefore sought an interview with Chandra Rao to give him sound advice, but was treacherously taken captive by the latter and had to make good his escape by skilful daring. Shivaji could no longer put up with the hostile conduct of Chandra Rao and sent his faithful officers, Ragho Ballal and Sambhaji Kavji, to Jaoli with a view of securing terms of submission from Chandra Rao, but had an altercation with him, which resulted in his death in 1655. Shivaji, who was watching the movements of his agents from Mahabaleshwar, marched at once to Jaoli with his troops, and fought with the two sons of Chandra Rao and his minister, Hanmant Rao (Grant Duff's Himmat Rao), who made a gallant resistance, but were ultimately defeated and captured by Shivaji. Hanmant Rao was killed in this action; and the two sons, Baji Rao and Krishna Rao, were taken prisoners and kept in the fort of Chakan. Shivaji, in his conquest of Jaoli, was greatly assisted by the brothers and relations of Chandra Rao, whose services he recognised by giving them due rewards and releasing their watans which were confiscated by Chandra Rao. A sanad granted to Krishnaji Yeshwant Rao More in Rajshak 28 A.D. (1712) supports the fact that Yeshwant Rao, brother of Chandra Rao, rendered valuable help to Shivaji in this affair. In the old chronicles, mention is made of a traditional saying "मिळाले बारा भाई आणि बुडविली चंद्रराई," *i.e.* "twelve brothers joined together and caused the downfall of *Chandra Rai*" (kingdom of Chandra Rao); which shows that family dissensions were at the bottom of this occurrence.

Shivaji, after the conquest of Jaoli, succeeded in securing the possessions of the late Chandra Rao in a short time, and subdued the country upto Panhala and Southern Konkan. He utilised the immense treasures of Chandra Rao in improving the temples of Mahabaleshwar and building the fort of Pratapgad, which gave general satisfaction to the descendants of Mores, and widened his fame and popularity in that country.*

After establishing his rule in the hilly country of Jaoli and Mahabaleshwar, Shivaji lost no time in enlisting in his infantry the brave Mawlis who were in the service of Chandra Rao, and in fortifying strong positions in his new dominion. He entrusted the work of training the Mawlis to Netaji Palker

---

* Grant Duff, in his admirable History of the Marathas, has charged Shivaji and his officers with assassination, in narrating the downfall of Chandra Rao. The account given by Grant Duff from the imperfect and scanty materials, then available to him, requires modification in the light of more authentic and reliable documents that have lately been discovered. They give altogether a different version of the incident and exonerate Shivaji from the charge of murder.

and of building the fortifications to Moro Trimal Pingle, both being young men of great promise and uncommon capacity. In 1656, to secure access to his possessions on the banks of the Nira and the Koyana and to defend the passes in the Konkan, he selected a high and commanding rock, west of Mahabaleshwar, for erecting a new fort. Par Ghaut, which leads the old route into the Konkan, winding up a very steep incline with so many curves that it was named by the British, 'the Corkscrew Pass,' was considered very important and highly strategic; and to secure its defence, Moro Trimal Pingle erected a strong fortress over this hill, which was named 'Pratapgad,' or 'the Fort of Glorious Exploits,' which made Shivaji's power formidable. When this fort was completed, Shivaji built temples to Kedareshwar and Ramvardayini Devi, the family deities of Chandra Rao More, and distributed charities to the Brahmins of Mahabaleshwar, who were then reputed to be pious, learned and well versed in the Vedas. Ramdas Swami, the Guru or spiritual preceptor of Shivaji, was present at this time at Mahabaleshwar. Shivaji highly valued this new fortress and considered it a key to further conquests.

AFZUL KHAN.

The Bijapur government, awakened by the significant deeds of Shivaji in the Konkan and on the Ghauts, saw the necessity of making a supreme effort to subdue him. They therefore resolved to send a strong army against Shivaji, and appointed Afzul Khan, a famous general of Bijapur, to its command. The expedition of Afzul Khan against Shivaji was a momentous event in the history of the Marathas, and has been described by Grant Duff at some length. He appears to have relied more on Persian *tawarikhs* than on original Marathi *bakhars*. The authentic version of this historical episode as given in a Marathi *bakhar* written by the Shedgaonkar Bhonsles, descendants of Sharfoji, Shivaji's uncle, and preserved in the Satara Palace, appears to be more reliable.* From that account, it is evidently clear that Afzul Khan, who in open darbar proudly professed that he would return to Bijapur with the insignificant and impudent rebel Shivaji in chains, was more than a match for Shivaji. He started from Bijapur, early in 1659, with an armed force fully equipped with guns and rockets, a number of swivels mounted on camels, and ample stores. On his way having desecrat-

* See the extract of this *bakhar* published in the 'Itihas Sangraha.' Vol. VI., Nos. 4-5-6, page 62.

ed the well-known Hindu temples of Pandharpur and Tuljapur and having broken their idols, he reached Wai and encamped with his huge army in the fertile Krishna valley. Shivaji perceived the gravity of the situation and prepared to face it boldly. He invoked the Goddess Bhavani, and favoured with her divine blessings, resolved to meet his great enemy. He did not intend to risk a battle but took up a position at Pratapgad. Afzul Khan, who was proud of his large army and almost certain that Shivaji could not face him in the field, was bent upon catching him in his mountain shelter and taking him in triumph to Bijapur. Shivaji perceiving the difficult situation made offers of submission to the Khan, who deputed his confidential agent, Krishnaji Bhaskar, to open negotiations with Shivaji. This man was gained over by Shivaji through Pantoji Gopinath Bokil, and with his assistance Afzul Khan was easily led to believe that Shivaji was in a state of great alarm and willing to surrender, provided pardon was granted to him for his past actions. The Khan, aware of the natural difficulties of the mountainous country, in spite of his hatred and contempt for his foe, consented to accept Shivaji's submission in a personal interview. Shivaji knew the Khan's physical strength as well as his real motive. He therefore implored Krishnaji Bhaskar to bring the Khan to the place of meeting without any attendants. The Khan acceded to this request. Dressed in a plain muslin robe, he came to the interview in a palanquin armed with a straight sword, accompanied by one attendant, named Syed Banda. Shivaji, taking into consideration the seriousness of the occasion, wore a steel cap under his turban, a chain armour beneath his cotton gown, concealed a dagger in his right sleeve, and fastened on the fingers of his left hand, *wagh-nakhs* or tiger-claws (sharp hooks of steel that lie concealed in the closed hand). Thus prepared for any emergency, he slowly descended from the fort. The Khan arrived from the valley below in his palanquin to the spot, which was richly decorated and specially fitted for the memorable interview. In the customary embrace, it is stated in the Marathi chronicles, the stalwart Khan first seized Shivaji's neck with his left hand and struck him with the sword.* As soon as the Khan's treacherous object was mani-

* Extract from the Satara Bakhar, 'Itihas Sangrah,' Vol. VI, Nos. 4-5-6. page 70, and also Marathi Bakhars by Chitnis, Sabhasad and others.

fested, Shivaji plunged his *wagh-nakhs* into the side of the Khan in self-defence.

The Mamomedan chroniclers charge Shivaji with treachery, and allege that it was Shivaji who first struck Afzul Khan fiercely in the stomach with the concealed tiger-claws, and despatched him with an expeditious blow of the dagger, before the Khan could recover himself from his surprise. Thus, the Hindu and Mahomedan chroniclers differ vastly in their accounts. Consequently, all attempts at disinterring the truth from under the debris of racial prejudices are bound to failure more or less complete. Besides, it may be borne in mind, that when two capable and ambitious political opponents, suspicious of each other's motives and determined to nonplus each other, meet in a secret conference and one of them is found dead and the other remaining almost unscathed, it is the survivor who is generally accused of treachery. At any rate that is the fate of Shivaji. One cannot, however, help remarking that the Shivaji-Afzul Khan episode is one of those historical mysteries that bid fair to remain unsolved till the end of time.

The success of Shivaji in the combat against Afzul Khan raised him to the position of a national hero; the

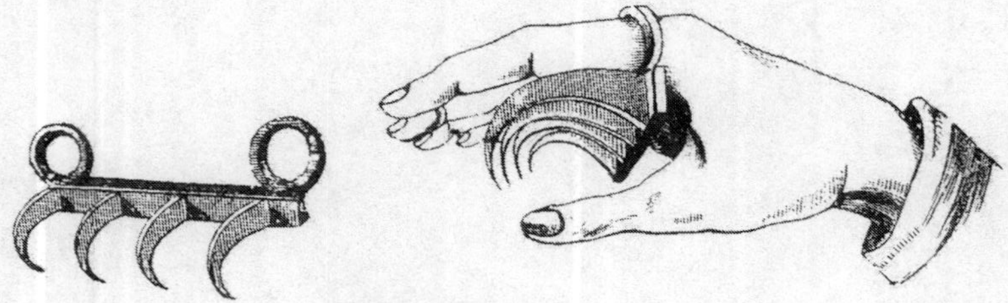

WAGHNAKHS OR TIGER-CLAWS.

(With which Shivaji killed Afzul Khan in A.D. 1659.)

sword and the *wagh-nakhs*, with which he killed Afzul Khan, are worshipped to this day by his descendants. "That very tiger's claw," writes Sir Richard Temple, late Governor of Bombay, "that very sword, that very coat of mail, that very muslin dress, are to this day religiously preserved from generation to generation by the Marathas. Never were the sword or the hat or any of the relics of Napolean or Frederick the Great of Prussia venerated so much by the French or Germans, as these relics of Shivaji are to this day by the Marathas."* "He (Shivaji) was," says Sir Edward Sullivan, another well-known English author, "almost worshipped as a god, and the renown of his deeds, his eagle glances and long arms, his rapid marches and secret forays, are to this day the most popular themes of the wandering Gursees, or minstrels of the Deccan. Even his weapons were reverenced as holy, and his good sword Bhowanee has been to the bards of the Deccan, what the Joyeuse and Duranel of Charlemagne and Roland, and the Askalon of our own patron saint, were to the wandering troubadours of Europe."†

---

* Oriental Experience by Sir Richard Temple, p. 366.

† Princes of India by Sir Edward Sullivan, p. 460.

After the death of Afzul Khan, Shivaji's men attacked and routed the Bijapur army. It is worthy of note that Shivaji, on this occasion, showed great kindness and humanity to the prisoners and gave them honourable treatment. It was indeed a gracious act on the part of Shivaji to have erected a tomb over the remains of Afzul Khan and built a tower in his honour, which is still known by the name 'Afzul Buruj' at Pratapgad. The sword of Afzul Khan was preserved as a valued trophy in the armoury of Shivaji and his descendants. The golden cones of his tent were presented to the temple of the God Mahabaleshwar, and their lustre yet shines brilliantly through the charming hills in the neighbourhood.

Shivaji built a large temple at Pratapgad in A.D. 1661, and dedicated it to the Goddess Bhavani with great solemnity and religious ceremonies. A new image of this Goddess was carved out of a black stone specially brought from Nepal by Shivaji's agent Sonawani, for which he was granted the hereditary right of protecting the temple. The old image of Ramwardayini Devi belonging to Chandra Rao More was returned to his descendants, who removed it to the village of Par and enshrined it there.

VIEW OF THE AFZUL BURUJ AT PRATAPGAD.

Shivaji and his descendants held the deities, Bhavani and Mahabaleshwar, in great veneration, and sent annually, valuable offerings and presents to the temples at Pratapgad and Mahabaleshwar. Raja Shahu, on his return from the Mogul court, paid a visit to these temples in 1712, and took considerable interest in their improvement. After the death of Raja Shahu in 1749, his ministers, the Peshwas, established themselves independently at Poona, and his descendants were confined in the fortress at Satara as the shadows of a great house. The hills of Mahabaleshwar and Pratapgad were under the *subha* of Jaoli. The fort of Pratapgad was used by the Peshwas as a political prison, where they had kept Sakharam Bapu Bokil as a state-prisoner in 1779. It may be remarked here that the ancestor of this man, Pantoji Gopinath, took a prominent part in the tragedy of Afzul Khan's death, exactly 120 years before. On the downfall of the Peshwa's rule in 1818, the fort was taken by the British Government into their possession, and the hills of Mahabaleshwar were included in the territory, which was restored to Shivaji's descendant, Raja Pratap Sing of Satara. It must be said to the credit of the British Government that they respected the religious susceptibilities of the Marathas while the fort of Pratapgad was in their possession till 1824. They guarded the temple and did not allow unauthorised persons to enter it. It was Captain Grant (then Resident at Satara and afterwards the famous historian Grant Duff) who wrote on the 19th November 1819, to Col. Kennedy, Commanding Southern Konkan:—"There is a temple of Bhavani in Pratapgad which is held particularly sacred by the Marathas and especially by the descendants of Shivaji. I have therefore to beg that you will have the goodness to order a sentry to be placed near it, in order to prevent all persons from entering it, who may not be authorised to do so by the officiating Brahmins." The regard and respect shown by the British Government to the temples at Pratapgad and Mahabaleshwar speak highly of their magnanimity and religious toleration.

GODDESS BHAVANI OF PRATAPGAD.

CHAPTER II.

THE SANITARIUM:

NAHAR OR MALCOLM PETH.

(Its Inception).

IT is generally believed that the first European gentleman, who ever set foot on the Mahabaleshwar hills, was General Lodwick. He made known the salubrity of their climate, and led to the establishment of the Mahabaleshwar Sanitarium which conferred an inestimable benefit on the Bombay Presidency. For this great discovery, the memory of General Lodwick has been perpetuated this day, by naming a popular and prominent point on these hills after him, and raising a fitting monument there in his honour. But the true history of the establishment of this hill-station is yet in obscurity, though attempts have been made in recent years by inquisitive scholars to find out reliable information from different sources. It will, therefore, not be out of place, if an attempt is made to give here a succinct and trustworthy account of the foundation of the Mahabaleshwar Sanitarium from authentic and original sources, and bring to light new facts that are hidden in the dark.

It has been already mentioned in the first chapter that the sacred Hindu village of Mahabaleshwar, which is called '*Kshetra* Mahabaleshwar,' or the holy place of Mahabaleshwar, was well-known to the people of Maharashtra and was visited by them in *Kanyagat*—when Jupiter is in the sign of Virgo, once every twelve years. Shivaji, the founder of the Maratha empire, and his revered mother Jijabai, showed much reverence to this place, and made endowments to the temple and gave *varshasans* or annual grants to the learned Brahmins of this holy place. Shivaji's descendants, as well as the Peshwas and all the Maratha Sardars, visited this place on pilgrimage, and bathed in the holy waters of the Krishna on eclipses and auspicious days. The Peshwa, Sawai Madhav Rao, and his famous minister, Nana Phadnavis, paid a visit to this place in the years 1791, which important event is recorded in the Peshwas' Diaries that are carefully preserved in the Poona Daftar by the British Government. The date of the Peshwa's visit to Mahabaleshwar is given as

छ १५ सफर इसन्ने तिसैन मया व अलफ, which corresponds to the 14th October A.D. 1791. On this date, there is an entry in the Peshwa's diary, that Rs. 17½ were spent in charity at Mahabaleshwar.

It is a note-worthy fact that in this memorable trip, the Peshwa was accompanied by Sir Charles Malet, the first British Resident at the Poona Darbar, with his suite. Major Price, a military officer, who formed part of the Resident's escort, has made the following mention in his "Memoirs":—

"12th October—An eclipse of the moon, which took place some time this morning, occasioned the celebration of the Jatra (Yatra or festival) at Mahabaliser or Mahabaliswara, said to be among the hills about eight Kosse (16 miles) to the westward. This festival, it is said, does not otherwise occur more than once in a cycle of twelve years.

"14th October—This afternoon the young Peshwa, accompanied by a numerous suvary (swaree) or cavalcade, left his camp for Mahabaliser.

"Contrary to what I had been formerly led to conceive, that the Krishna, at its source, issued from separate springs, I was now apprized that there are five distinct rivers, which take their rise near the same fountain head; some of which bend their course into the Konkan, or territory below the Ghauts; and particularly that which enters the sea at Bankote, or fort Victoria.

"The village Mahabaliser, at the source of the Krishna, lay, as already intimated, on the eastern slope of the mountain; and was barely visible when pointed out by one acquainted with the spot, and one large pagoda was clearly distinguished through telescope.

"Although in itself a trifle, I could not omit to mention the pleasing surprise with which I discovered several patches of common fern on different parts of the elevated spot, on which we were enjoying the freshness of the mountain breeze, and the variegated landscape on every side, destitute, however, of every vestige of that forest scenery so essential to the picturesque, the hills being entirely naked of wood. I could almost have compared my surprise at the sight of a single fern plant, to that of Robinson Crusoe, when he discovered the print of a human foot on the strand. Mine, however, was the surprise of an indefinable pleasure, that of poor Crusoe was one of terror and alarm."*

* The Memoirs of a Field Officer by Major Price.

From these extracts it appears that the Peshwa visited the sacred shrine of Mahabaleshwar, and the Resident, Sir Charles Malet, with his staff, accompanied him. Nana Phadanvis, the astute minister of the Peshwa, who was present in this trip, communicated this important event to Haripant Phadake, the Commander-in-Chief of the Maratha army. His letter clearly shows that Sir Charles Malet had been to Mahabaleshwar with the Peshwa. This interesting document is in Marathi and its translation is given below:—

"The Peshwa and his retinue came to Wai, and after the eclipse, went on the 3rd Ashwin *Vadya* (dark half of Ashwin) to Mahabaleshwar and returned on the 4th. Malet accompanied him. Malet always goes 4 or 5 koss daily in search of sport. There are many forts here, and he examines them daily through a telescope. He then draws plans of them. * * *"

This document proves beyond doubt the fact that Malet visited the Mahabaleshwar hills in the company of the Peshwa in 1791. It therefore strongly supports his claim to be called the first European explorer of the Mahabaleshwar hills. Since that time the name of Mahabaleshwar became known to Europeans in Western India and gradually attracted their notice. In 1820, Walker Hamilton, the father of the Indian Gazetteers, mentions Mahabaleshwar as one of the principal towns in the Satara territory, and further describes :—"At this place, distant 43 miles from the Western Coast of India, the river Krishna has its source, and from hence it travels the whole way across to the Bay of Bengal. The spot is of course much venerated by the Hindus."

Just before this period, great political events had taken place in Maharashtra, and the Peshwa's territories were conquered by the British. The generous and enlightened policy of Mr. Elphinstone, who was at the head of political affairs in the Deccan at this time, restored the Raja of Satara to his ancient Maratha throne, and endowed him with an independent sovereignty sufficient to maintain the name and dignity of the royal house of the great Shivaji. For several years the royal authority of the Satara dynasty had been practically set aside by the Peshwas, and its titular sovereign was then a prisoner in the hands of the last Peshwa, Baji Rao.

With a view to conciliate the Marathas, Mr. Elphinstone thought it prudent to create a new principality for the descendant of Shivaji,—a measure which was

RAJA PRATAP SING.

(Raja of Satara, A.D. 1818-1839.)

highly commended by statesmen of those days and which proved to be a great success. At the termination of the Maratha War, the Raja of Satara was placed on the throne with great pomp, on the 11th of April 1818, and a treaty of alliance and friendship was concluded between the Raja and the British Government on the 25th September 1819. Under this treaty, the territory ceded to the Raja comprised the compact and fertile tract lying on the western border of the Deccan, between the Nira and the Bhima rivers on the north, and the Warna and the Krishna to the south; and extending from the Western Ghauts eastward to the Districts of Bijapur and Pandharpur. It yielded a revenue of from 14 to 15 lacs of Rupees, and was noted for the salubrity of its climate, the Mahabaleshwar hills being only thirty miles distant from Satara, the Raja's capital.

A short account of this newly created Maratha sovereign will not be considered out of place here, especially as he was greatly instrumental in bringing about the establishment of this popular hill-station. "The Rajah Pertab Sing," writes General Briggs, the second Resident at Satara, "was twenty-four years of age when he was installed as a ruling Raja of Satara. Owing to the rigid seclusion in which he had been kept from his birth under the power of the Peshwa, and his being wholly unused to business, it was determined that his country should, for a time, be under English management. It was thought right not only that the British Government should be satisfied of His Highness's capacity and disposition, but also that means should be taken to disabuse his mind of the exaggerated pretensions to supremacy over all the Marathas, encouraged by his mother and other relations. With this view, Captain Grant (afterwards Grant Duff), who was intimately acquainted with the Maratha customs and languages, was appointed Resident, with full power to conduct the administration under instructions from the Sole Commissioner, Mr. Elphinstone, who furnished a complete code of rules by which the government was to be conducted; a civil list, equal to one-fifth of the revenue, being assigned to the Raja and his family." The Raja being naturally very intelligent and clever, soon got insight into the administration under the able and friendly guidance of Captain Grant, who trained him in the principles and details of government and sufficiently acquainted him with a practical knowledge of the world. He not only instructed him in the art of administration, but cultivated in him a higher taste for literary and general knowledge and education, and instilled into his mind the importance of virtue and character. This close intercourse of the Raja with a highly cultured English gentleman had a wonderful effect on his Oriental mind; and he at once turned out a most refined and excellent ruler. "He (the Raja)," writes Hon. Mr. Elphinstone in 1826, "is the most civilized Maratha I ever met with, has his country in excellent order, and everything to his roads and aqueducts in a style that would do credit to a European. I was more struck with his private sitting room than anything I saw at Satara. It contains a single table covered with green velvet, at which the descendant of Shivaji sits in a chair and writes letters as well as a journal of his transactions with his own hand. I do not know what his ancestor would think of so peaceful a descendant."* It was all due to the Western training the Raja had received from the Resident. It widened his vision so that he could see the advantages of literature, science, art and industry, which enabled him to

* Life of Mountstuart Elphinstone, Vol. II, page 188.

achieve better results in the administration of his own State, and won for him the good will and gratitude of his subjects, and admiration and praise from the Paramount Power.* It was the enlightened mind of the Raja that quickly perceived the benefits of a sanitarium in his own State, and readily offered his co-operation and help in its establishment.

Captain Grant or Grant Duff was Resident at Satara from 1818 to 1822. He was an able and efficient officer and possessed all the qualities that were necessary for a Resident in those days. In addition to judgment, energy and talents for business of no ordinary kind, he possessed in an eminent degree, the power of appreciating the character of the people and adopting measures to suit their peculiarities, which made him popular with the Raja and his rayats alike. The name

---

* An eminent authority on Satara writes in the "Calcutta Review" :—

"The administration of the country continued for a series of years to be the subject of general admiration. It was pre-eminent among Native States for the general mildness and equity of its rule and for the utility and extent of its public works. The traveller, as he passed through the Satara Territory, bore witness to the prosperity of the country and contentment of the people. Successive Governors, who visited the Raja's Court, were favourably impressed with his character and testified their high admiration of his rule, and the Home Authorities cordially re-echoed their tribute of praise."—*Calcutta Review*, Vol. X, page 442.

"Grant Saheb" is still familiar as a household word in the Satara District. Before he finally left the Residency, he invested the Raja with full powers, and also secured for him the historical fortress of Pratapgad, which was still in the possession of the British Government. The famous temple of Bhavani, the family Goddess of Shivaji and his descendants, being situated on this fortress, the Raja was extremely anxious to have it included in his own territory. On the recommendation of Grant Duff, the exemplary conduct of the Raja was taken into consideration by the British Government, and the fortress was ceded to him in 1823 as a mark of favour. This act of generosity on the part of the British Government pleased the Raja immensely; and with feelings of gratitude and joy, and religious devotion, he at once undertook a journey to Pratapgad and paid his respects to the Goddess on the 24th April 1823.* The Raja, who went

---

* The Raja's letter to Grant Duff describing this important event is dated the 26th April 1823 and is given below:—

"In conformity to your arrangement concerning the fortress of Pratapgar, to be ceded by the British Government to this Sirkar, it has been delivered over to me; and I had the pleasure of undertaking a pilgrimage to that place. I arrived here on the 12th of Shaban or 24th April, and having visited the Goddess, returned to Satara. I have been highly gratified on this occasion, which you will be glad to learn by this."

alone on this journey, was greatly delighted to see the Goddess Bhavàni and the historical fortress of Pratapgad and its neighbourhood, which had a magical effect on his orthodox mind. He was so much impressed with them that he resolved to go there next year with his brother, Shahaji alias Appa Saheb, and his family, in state.

The Raja's second visit to Pratapgad in March A.D. 1824 was an event of great consequence. The descendant of Shivaji going on a pilgrimage to the famous temple of Bhavani naturally aroused the curiosity and enthusiasm of his loyal subjects; and the people of Pratapgad and its surrounding places were eager to receive him with the respect due to his exalted position. The Raja's camp consisting of more than 2,000 followers of every shape and rank, spread for miles, over hill and dale. There were numerous tents, flags, horses and elephants. In fact, it was a scene of magnificent splendour. The Raja went to Pratapgad by the old route in the hilly country and passed through the picturesque mountains of Mahabaleshwar. On his return, he ascended the Mahabaleshwar hills, and pitched his camp on the place, called डेरियाचा माळ (Mal of royal tents),

GENERAL JOHN BRIGGS.

(Resident at Satara, A. D. 1823-1826.)

still known as the 'Raja's camping ground' near the present Race Course. It is noted in his diary, that he halted at this place on the 12th March 1824, distant 6 Koss (12 miles) from Pratapgad.

At this time Colonel (afterwards General) John Briggs was Resident at Satara, who succeeded Grant Duff in January 1823. He was a great scholar and a very affable and kind-hearted gentleman. He had gladly accepted the Residency of Satara, as it offered a healthier climate and somewhat more of society to his wife and children and more leisure to himself for study and literary pursuits. He had three Civilians to assist him in the Residency, namely, Messrs. Houlton, Montgomerie and Shaw. Surgeon Conwell and Assistant Surgeon Kane were the Medical Officers under him; and Major Peter Lodwick, with Captain Mathews and Lieutenant Smith, commanded the Native Infantry Regiment stationed at Satara. Besides these, there was Captain Adams doing the special Survey duty in the service of the Raja. These chiefly formed the European society at Satara. On the Raja's return from Pratapgad, Colonel Briggs and Major Lodwick were much interested to learn the account of his trip, and took a fancy to see these mountain places in the same hot season. Major Lodwick was then actually suffering from the effects of heat in the plains and was in need of change. He therefore welcomed the idea most heartily and arranged an excursion party to the hills. Colonel Briggs does not appear to have joined the party. Lodwick and other juniors, civil and military, numbering six, carried out their plan in April 1824. Their trip proved afterwards to be a note-worthy event in the history of Mahabaleshwar, inasmuch as it brought to light the salubrious climate, the picturesque scenery, the high elevation and the excellent water of these hills,—the chief conditions that go to make a good sanitarium. Major Lodwick on his return to Satara from Mahabaleshwar wrote a letter to the "Bombay Courier" over the signature "L," and placed before the public the experiences of his visit to the newly discovered land, which created a good deal of sensation in those days. The letter runs thus:—

To,

THE EDITOR OF "THE BOMBAY COURIER."

Mr. Editor,

That we are all prone to neglect the comforts and enjoyments within our reach, while eagerly anticipating those which are difficult of attainment, is an observation which every day's experience renders more evident without correcting the error —for such is the nature of man; and he, who is unhappy and unwell from his own disposition or his habits of business or idleness, considers that a return to his native land, can alone and will assuredly render him both healthy and happy. I wish not to destroy the illusion; but it is my firm belief that, in most cases, climate has less effect than a change of habits, both as to exercise and the extended practice of the social affections.

Confined to the routine of an office, or the idleness of a cantonment, and every day nearly of similar tenor, the mind in India loses by degrees the tone of healthy action, the body suffers in consequence, and we have no Bath or Cheltenham, as at home, where freedom from care and enjoyment of a large and gay society generally performs those cures which are attributed to the virtues of their far famed springs.

I have been led into these reflections by a residence during last month at Mahabillysir, one of the highest of our own Deccan Hills, with a party which, from our proximity to a station, fluctuated in number from two to six; and having derived from the excursion, both enjoyment and improved health, I hope, through the means of your widely circulated paper to induce some of your readers, whose health and spirits are on the decline, to try a residence here, previous to incurring the heavy expenses and suffering the misery of two sea voyages; and can venture to promise them, even in the month of April, a climate in which the days are never sultry and the nights always cold, not that chilling cold, arising from dense vapour of the plains; but a bracing cold, peculiar to mountains, which gives elasticity both to body and mind.

I send a journal of the Thermometer from the day of my arrival to that of my departure; it was kept in a tent fully exposed, which we referred to the shelter of a Tope of trees in our rear; and no one of our party regretted the arrangement or thought of seeking its shelter. In fact, with the exception of an occasional short lull between the breezes, we were in the constant enjoyment of coolness—frequently cold when the Thermometer was at 72°, nor was it oppressive at 86°, as the air was sharp and bracing.

The river Jenna (Yenna) ran at our feet and afforded the advantage of cold bathing. Our supplies came in one night from Satara, distant 28 miles, the high-roads to Bombay and Whye (Wai) enabled us to take horse-exercise and game of every description encouraged walking over the Hills.

The scenery from many positions is both grand and romantic, reminding one of old England, from the ground being covered with high fern, the wild, rich note of the black-bird (common to the highest Deccan Hills) meeting the ear on every side, while the eye looked down upon the Ghauts and over the Conkan to the ocean.

Neither tigers nor thieves are to be feared; we neither saw nor heard of any during our stay.

With these advantages, a never failing appetite and high spirits without lassitude after strong exercise, or ennui without it, at this season of the year, insure these blessings in a much higher degree at any other period from October, when the monsoon closes, and visitors may calculate upon seven or eight months' enjoyment of as delightful a climate as can be desired.

There is abundant room for several parties who may be near or distant from each other and Mahabillysir is capable of becoming from its centrical situation the resource of all who are in search of health, of pleasure, or of retirement, without much fear of disappointment and with power of returning home immediately, should duty call or expectation not be gratified.

SATARA, Yours Obediently,
May 1st 1824.

L.

For some time after the publication of the above letter nothing of importance occurred, as Major Lodwick was immediately ordered to proceed on a military expedition to Kittur, a small State in the Karnatic, where some disturbances had occurred. He left Satara in June 1824, and did not return there till he was appointed Resident at Satara by the Honourable the Earl of Clare, Governor of Bombay, in 1832.

Major Lodwik's letter to the "Courier," gave, no doubt, wide publicity to the discovery of the unknown Mahabaleshwar hills, and soon attracted considerable attention of the public. As a result of it, perhaps, another enterprising traveller undertook a journey to this place immediately after Lodwick, in November 1824. He was the famous Reverend Gordon Hall, the founder of the American Mission in Southern India and author of the Marathi translation of the New Testament. He has written a journal of his tour to the Ghauts, wherein he mentions to have seen the summit of Par Ghaut, "where Major and party pitched their tents last hot season." He further describes:—"This spot as a climate is charming, and the prospect to the West very attractive, though little else than immense region of innumerable barren hills wildly crowded together meets the eye. To the East, North, and South, as far as the eye can reach, nothing can be seen but mountains far more towering and majestic, but equally desolate in appearance." He also visited the holy and secluded spot, now called 'Old Mahabaleshwar.'

The year 1825 is remarkable in the history of Mahabaleshwar, as it brought the distinguished visitor, Colonel Briggs, to these hills, on the 10th of May. The Colonel, it may be observed, was a most capable and talented officer and a true admirer of natural scenery. He had earned golden opinions of Elphinstone for his political sagacity, military valour and scholarship. No sooner did he set foot on these hills and see all the advantages bestowed by nature there, than he conceived high ideas of utilising them for the benefit of humanity. He remained there only for a month or two, but was greatly charmed by the romantic scenery and the bracing climate of that place. Being attached to the Madras Army, he had on many an occasion seen the Nilgiri Hills, which were then highly talked of as very likely to be made a sanitarium for European invalids in India, and had attracted considerable attention of Government. Colonel Briggs, therefore, noted with care all the prospective advantages of Mahabaleshwar, if it were made a sanitarium for the Bombay Presidency. On his coming back to Satara, he tried to impress them on the mind of the Raja, and induced him to make a good road to Mahabaleshwar as it was essential for communication. The Raja being shrewd enough to understand the importance of the Resident's suggestions readily promised him co-operation and help. It is noted in the Raja's diary on the 22nd August 1825:—" Colonel Briggs in his interview with His Highness recommended him to repair Par Ghaut and make a road from Satara via Medha and Radtondi Ghaut upto Mahad, and keep a ferry boat on the river Yenna, to which His Highness agreed, and said that it would make the country prosperous and increase the trade."

After the rains were over, the Raja commenced the work of constructing a new road to Pratapgad from Satara via Medha and Kelghar, but no appreciable progress was made till the summer of 1826. The Raja had been to Jejuri to pay a friendly visit to the Honourable Mr. Elphinstone, the Governor of the Presidency, and perhaps this might have hampered the progress of the work. But the tenacious Resident did not remain silent. He accompanied the Raja to Mahabaleshwar in April 1826 and personally undertook to supervise the work of construction. In the Raja's diary we find it stated that, on the 21st April, the Raja supplied Colonel Briggs 800 coolies (the wages being Rs. 4 a month) and Rs. 15,000 for the expenses of improving the Par Ghaut alone. In another place in the same diary, it is mentioned that the Colonel proposed to the Raja to spend Rs. 5,000 in constructing a dam on the river Yenna at Mahabaleshwar. From these references it is evident that Colonel Briggs and the Raja worked hand in hand for the development of this place. In 1826 Colonel Briggs built a small wooden house* for himself on the Sindola Hill and stayed there with his family. His son, known to the people by the name, "Chota Brigg," was with him. The Raja had his camp on the Deria's Mal. He afterwards built a spacious bungalow for himself. While Colonel Briggs had succeeded in securing the hearty co-operation and sympathy of the Raja of Satara to carry out his laudable object, he did not fail to draw the attention of his own Government to it. He urged the claims of Mahabaleshwar to be a fit sanitarium for the Bombay Presidency on its wise ruler, the Honourable Mr. Elphinstone, and at his desire submitted in 1826 to the Medical Board of Bombay, a detailed report on the subject of the climate and other local advantages of this place. The report runs thus :—

* The first cottage that was built at Mahabaleshwar in 1826 by Col. Briggs, then Resident at Satara, was in the possession of Sir James Dewar in 1830. It afterwards passed through several hands and it has now become very difficult to identify it. It is however supposed that it was near the Sindola Hill.

To

THE PRESIDENT AND MEMBERS OF THE
MEDICAL BOARD, BOMBAY.

GENTLEMEN,

In conformity with instructions conveyed to me from Government through the Chief Secretary under date the 9th instant, I do myself the honour to address you on the subject of the climate and local advantages of the table-land of Mahbleshwar as a resort for European invalids.

In conveying his instructions, the Chief Secretary also forwarded to me an extract from a letter from Mr. Sullivan, the Collector of Coimbatore in the Madras Provinces, addressed to Mr. Warden, which gave cover to two medical reports selected from a number of others on the same subject, drawn up by Doctor Wyse and Doctor Haines, on the climate and other advantages possessed by the Nilgherry Hills favourable to the European constitution.

The result of these reports and of the experience afforded by the residence of Mr. Sullivan and several gentlemen who have visited those mountains, whether for their health or as professional men, has been, it appears, a determination on the part of the Madras Government to erect suitable buildings for the accommodation of invalids, both officers and privates, whom it may be thought desirable to send there, and, it seems the intention of the Bombay Government in requiring me to correspond with you on this subject to endeavour to ascertain whether or not the Mahbleshwar Hills in the territory of the Rajah of

Sattara offer advantages for Europeans of the Bombay Establishment equal to those of Nilgherry.

In viewing this question it will not be improper to advert in the first place to the nature of the climates generally of the territories of Madras and Bombay, before we proceed to the second question of the comparative advantages of Mahbleshwar and Nilgherry. From an experience of many years' residence in the Madras Provinces, I may venture to assert that with the exception of Mysore in which territory but a small part of the establishment is fixed, the climate is everywhere extremely hot throughout the year, and from April to October it is most oppressive to the European constitution. The rain which commences in the latter month and ceases in December brings some temporary relief; but at no period of the year does the air possess such freshness as to invigorate the European frame or to renovate it from the languid produced by the constant heat. This heat however is equable, and as little variation takes place, I believe fever prevails less than on this side of India, while all complaints originating in diseased liver, and which are productive of general debility and exhaustion are more frequent. It seems natural, therefore, that a bracing climate like that of Nilgherry should be highly appreciated, and the great advantages it possesses from its local position, situated as it is within the Madras territory, tend to render it peculiarly fitted for the object to which it seems to be destined.

My own experience of several years of the Deccan and Candeish climates together with the information your Board must possess of that of Guzerat and of the whole territory subject to the Bombay Presidency, facilitates a comparison of these climates with that of Madras. The very circumstance of the rainy season occurring on this side of the Peninsula at the time when the sun is nearly verticle, and its continuance till near the autumnal equinox limit the period of hot weather to about three months, *viz.*, March, April and May. The sudden variations of the temperature of the air after the rains, till the return of the sun north at the vernal equinox, seems to induce fever complaints in various shapes, more or less, in almost all parts of the Bombay establishment according to local circumstances, notwithstanding which your Board will be disposed to admit, I have no doubt, that from June till February (nine months of the year) the climate of the Deccan on the whole is not only not baneful to the European constitution, but I am taught to believe Poona in particular at that period affords an example of salubrity among the European regiments almost unparalleled.

Having contrasted the relative climates of the Madras and Bombay territories, I shall revert to those of Nilgherry and Mahbleshwar. Of the former we have seen a register of the thermometer through the medium of the Madras papers for several years at different seasons, and, as I have before observed, the experience of the persons who have resided throughout the year on these mountains goes for to prove that with due preparations against cold the climate is decidedly healthy, and the temperature perhaps as congenial to the European constitution as can anywhere be met with.

Our experience of Mahbleshwar is hitherto very limited. Lieut.-Col. Lodwick having heard of its cool climate and suffering extremely from the heat in the months of April and May, was induced to give it a trial; and he with a small party of other gentlemen accordingly arrived on the 1st of April, and left Mahbleshwar finally on the 30th May 1824. In the year 1825 my own health induced me to make a similar trial, and I spent the greater part of April and May here, during which time a valetudinarian friend resided with me. Colonel Lodwick, myself and friend all derived so great a benefit from the climate that, on the occasion of two members of my family being taken ill at Sattara in the beginning of March last, I re-visited these hills and constructed a temporary bungalow for our own residence, where we have remained till this day, but the indications of the monsoon have now determined me to quit it. The register of the thermometer in the months of April and May, the two hottest in the year, (during the years, 1824, 25, 26) is forwarded with remarks on the weather generally from which an idea will at once be formed of its climate. The register indicates a temperature about 10° warmer than Nilgherry and from 15° to 20° cooler than either Sattara or Bancote on the Coast. During these months a cool refreshing breeze prevails throughout the day and night, and the only heat (which is never oppressive) occurs occasionally when the wind ceases, as it sometimes does for an hour or two, in the middle of the day. For the most part, however, the breeze is uniform, and on the whole more delightful climate cannot be desired; but a fair estimate of it throughout the year cannot be made without experience of the remaining ten months. The accounts, given by the inhabitants, collected from several sources, concur in representing that the monsoon usually commences in June, when thick mists and fogs prevail with much rain. Throughout its duration, the sun is but seldem seen, and it sometimes remains obscured for several days. The air at this time is chilly and damp but by no means unwholesome.

Colds, coughs and rheumatism even are not common, and fever is hardly known. The monsoon continues till September, after which the weather clears up and the air becomes gradually colder every day till February. During the months of December and January, the Natives describe the cold as intense, and they affirm with every probability of truth that hoar-frost is common at that season. I visited the hills early in February this year. The annual maximum of the heat of the thermometer in a tent at noon was 70° of Farenheit; and no inconvenience was felt by exposure to the sun, throughout the whole day. The local situation of Mahbleshwar is well described by one of our party whose account I perceive inserted in "the Bombay Courier" of the 27th instant, and to which I beg to refer you. He mentions its position as a table-land situated at 30 miles equidistant between Sattara and the town of Mharr on the Saweetry, the river debouching into the sea at Bankote. The elevation according to calculations from the mean of boiling water by three of Farenheits thermometers made by Pastorelli was 4,513 feet above the level of the sea, which nearly corresponds, I believe, with the trignometrical measurement. This height at 18th degree of North Latitude by no means promises so cool a climate, but it is known that temperature depends much on other circumstances as well as mere elevation. The surface of this table-land nowhere exceeding 10 miles in breadth frequently not above one or two, extends in length from 30 to 40 miles. The hills are for the most part covered with ferns but little jungle, it presents nowhere any extent of bare rock. The soil is reddish and sandy, poor, friable, and little disposed to adhesion, but retains moisture throughout the whole year within 12 or 15 inches of the surface. These facts seem all more or less calculated to prevent the sun operating powerfully, and the frequent exhalations in the shape of thin clouds and mists which are intercepted by these lofty regions, maintain the vegetable world in a state of constant verdure. A few Europe plants which usually wither at the same season in Sattara, have here flourished luxuriantly, and several cuttings and slips put down in March, not only took root but absolutely flowered before the end of May.

The rivers Yena, Quina and Krishna have their sources in the vicinity of the temple and village of

Mahbleshwar, and water of the finest quality is found in abundance in the numerous beautiful dells, overgrown with willows, and other ever-greens, which lead gradually from the mountains to the valleys below. Several advantageous positions present themselves for invalid stations, but the poverty of the soil offers so little inducement to the farmer that the cultivation is limited to the slopes of the mountains sheltered from the wind; and excepting four or five colonies of iron smelters, with here and there a small community of herdsmen, there are few other inhabitants on the table-land. The neighbouring vallies, however, are thickly studded with hamlets and villages, and the flourishing towns of Wayee, Merah (Medha) and Sattara, to the eastward with Par, Poladpoor and Marr (Mahad) to the west within the distance of eight, ten, twenty and thirty miles, afford ample resources which could at any time be concentrated and would furnish abundant supplies, if put in requisition.

His Highness the Rajah of Sattara with that spirit of improvement which charaterizes his Government, has in order to facilitate trade between the sea-coast and his capital, already commenced a road for that purpose, which passing through Merah from Sattara ascends the Kuroolsy Ghaut and leading near Mahbleshwar passes down the Rurtoondy Ghaut by Par and Purtabghur, to the top of the Par Ghaut, which conducts direct to Marr and Bankote. The improvement of this road has been made with the full expectation that the British Government will gladly unite the communication by making the road from the river to the top of the Par Ghaut. The whole of the Kuroolsy Ghaut and seven miles of the road along the table-land, have been already finished this year for the transport of carriages. During the rains the road from Sattara will be commenced on, and it is expected that before the commencement of the rainy season of 1827, the road throughout His Highness's territory will be completed.

Adverting to all the advantages, therefore, of the climate of these hills, with the facility of access which brings an invalid in four days from Bombay to this spot; to the delightful climate it possesses; to the beautiful and romantic scenery it presents in every direction; to the abundant supplies which might be brought from a short distance if measures be taken for that purpose; to the quantity of wood, and stone at hand for building; to the excellent road which is made, and the numerous cross-roads which might be made, at inconsiderable cost; it seems desirable at all events to give Mahbleshwar a trial, in preference to incurring all the inconveniences and expenses necessarily attendant on any project which should convert the Nilgherries into a general station for invalids, or convalescents of the Bombay establishment.

Upon the whole I am of opinion that the temperature of Mahbleshwar although warmer than that of Nilgherries possesses in that very circumstance an advantage over them. The transition frcm the Deccan atmosphere to Mahbleshwar is by no means so great as to cause any sudden alteration in the system, though an alteration certainly does occur, and while the constitution early accommodates itself to the change, it gradually recovers its tone from the freshness and exhilerating air the patient breathes, and the genial nature of an equable and temperate, though not cold climate.

In case a trial of this place is determined on, the beginning of the month of February perhaps for first year, might be fixed for the removal of the invalids, as upto that period, Bombay and the Deccan especially, have within themselves a cool climate. The sick should be supplied with warm clothing, bedding, and blankets, and comfortable tents, which shut close at night, with a fly and shell to each. Course country blankets and the means of hutting themselves comfortably, should also be afforded to the Native part of the establishment attending the sick. The experience of one season would probably be sufficient to enable Government to determine whether it was worthwhile to incur the expense of building hospitals, and in that case the permission of the Rajah's Government could, I imagine, be easily obtained for allotting such a portion of land for the purpose as might be found requisite.

For any further or particular information I beg to recommend the Board to apply to Dr. Bird, the Civil

Surgeon at the Residency, who has been in attendance on my family since March last at Mahbleshwar, and who is so competent in every respect to answer satisfactorily any queries which the Board may wish to put.

I have the honour to be
&c., &c., &c.,
(Sd.) JOHN BRIGGS,
Resident at Sattara.

MAHBLESHWAR,
31*st May*, 1826.

While Colonel Briggs was thus trying with Government to promote the good cause, another friend of his, styling himself 'Perambulator' published a letter in the "Bombay Courier" of the 20th May 1826, advertising to the public several climatic benefits of this beautiful hill, which considerably revived the public attention and elicited useful inquiries. All these efforts in the inception of a new health-resort reflected great credit on the energy, tact and public spirit of Colonel Briggs and his friend, the Raja of Satara, whose names ought to be cherished along with those of Lodwick and Malcolm. It was a matter of great pity that, shortly afterwards, Colonel Briggs, the real promoter of Mahabaleshwar, suffered from ill-health, and had to hand over the charge of his Residency as well as of his cherished scheme to Mr. William Simson, a young Civilian, in December 1826, and proceeded on leave to England on the 18th January 1827. He parted as a friend of the Raja, for whom he had "great respect for his many excellent qualities as a man and as a ruler."

CHAPTER III.

THE NEW SANITARIUM.

Its Establishment.

THE year 1827 did not seem favourable to the progress of the scheme, proposed by Colonel Briggs to the Government of the Hon'ble Mr. Elphinstone, regarding the establishment of a sanitarium at Mahabaleshwar. The able and detailed report submitted by Colonel Briggs to the Medical Board remained for some time under consideration; and the construction of the new road undertaken by the Raja of Satara was also delayed, probably owing to the changes in the personnel of the Resident as well as of the Governor. Mr. William Simson, who took over charge of the Satara Residency from Colonel Briggs in December 1826, on the latter's departure home on leave, acted for his successor, Lieutenant-Colonel Archibald Robertson, till June 1827. It appears, however, that during this short interval, the young gentleman took considerable interest in Mahabaleshwar. He secured the permission of the Raja to build a bungalow for the Resident on the Sindola Hill and actually commenced the work, which remained incomplete till December 1827.

This interval is memorable for its having witnessed a great public movement that kept the whole Presidency astir. A reference to it is needed here to make the situation more intelligible. It was not an agitation for political purposes. It was a public demonstration for expressing the true and loyal feelings of respect, esteem and admiration for the public and private virtues of a distinguished political personage, the Hon'ble Mr. Elphinstone, who exemplified in a signal manner the noble art which procures for the conqueror the truest glory—namely the art of gaining the attachment and love of the conquered people. There were several demonstrations all over the Deccan to express the sentiments of respect and good feeling, rarely bestowed on any functionary, and all classes of people took part in them. The public spirited Raja of Satara, being a personal friend and admirer of Elphinstone, took a leading part in this movement, and presented a learned address over his signature to the departing Governor. He also contributed liberally to the Memorial Fund, which was started to

SIR JOHN MALCOLM.
(Governor of Bombay, A. D. 1827-1830.)

perpetuate the good name of that great statesman. The present Elphinstone College is the happy outcome of that movement that made the name of Elphinstone imperishable in this country, and won for the Raja high praise and honour from all quarters.*

The new Governor, Sir John Malcolm, succeeded the Hon'ble Mr. Elphinstone on the 1st November 1827. He was highly distinguished for the noble qualities of a soldier and statesman, and was well-known for his esteem and attachment to the natives of this country. His advent was, therefore, considered, on all sides, most welcome and auspicious. On his arrival, Malcolm was delighted in nothing so much as in sounding the praises of his predecessor. He at once declared that he would adopt Elphinstone's policy and make no change in the administration.

---

* "I was very happy," writes Grant Duff to the Raja in 1828, "to see your name at the head of so excellent and proper an address as that presented to Mr. Elphinstone. The institution of a College for the purposes specified confers an honour on the Native Gentlemen of India, which if rightly followed up will last for ever. Your Highness, in consequence of this liberal act, has been appointed a Member of the Royal Asiatic Society of Great Britain and Ireland, which, no doubt, has been intimated to you. Col. Briggs, I am happy to learn, commends your administration exceedingly, and it is universally believed that no Native Prince ever governed his territory so well as Your Highness."

The Raja of Satara, who was already aware of the fame of Malcolm, took an early opportunity of sending his message of greetings and welcome to the new Governor, through his Resident, Lt.-Col. Robertson, and cordially invited him to Mahabaleshwar. It was a happy thing that the Raja had found in the new Resident a kind and generous friend, who possessed fine manners and an obliging disposition. He too was favourably impressed with the climate of Mahabaleshwar, and displayed similar interest and zeal in establishing a sanitarium there. It is noted in the Raja's diary that "he (the Resident) had an interview with His Excellency the Governor on 22nd December 1827, in which the latter made enquiries about the climate of Mahabaleshwar, and expressed a wish to visit the place and also see the Raja. The Raja was extremely pleased to learn of it."

The most noteworthy event in the annals of Mahabaleshwar is the first visit of the Governor of Bombay, which took place in May 1828. Sir John Malcolm with Dr. Williamson embarked from the new bunder of Bombay on the 27th April 1828, and arrived at Mahabaleshwar via Bankote and Mahad. Raja Pratap Sing of Satara and his Resident, Lt.-Col. Robertson, had made excellent arrangements for his reception and comfortable stay on the hills according to the means available in those days. The Governor put up at the Resident's bungalow on the Sindola Hill for the first time. The first glimpse of the hills made a favourable impression on his mind. The fascinating scenery, lovely climate and agreeable surroundings simply enchanted him. His sojourn on these hills was a happy augury of good results. It brought to his mind the advisability and importance of establishing a sanitarium on these hills. Sir John Malcolm immediately devoted his attention to the various suggestions received by Government in this respect. He ordered a survey to be made of these hills preparatory to the establishment of a hill station, and directed the Medical Board to appoint an expert to fully investigate the nature of the climate and its effects on invalids. In short, the first visit of the Governor gave much impetus to the scheme and produced good results in a short time. "We understand," writes "the Bombay Courier" on the 17th June 1828, "that one of the principal objects of the Governor's late visit to these hills was to obtain local information of the nature of the climate and of the advantages of the situation for establishing a convalescent station. The result of his inquiries has been highly satisfactory; and we hear, it is in the contemplation of Government to improve the road to it, and to afford every facility to the officers of the Presidency, who may be disposed to give a trial."

On his return from Mahabaleshwar, Sir John Malcolm selected Dr. Bird, Residency Surgeon at Satara, to ascertain the nature of the climate of the Mahabaleshwar hills. He asked the Resident of Satara, through his Secretary, Mr. William Newnham, whether Dr. Bird could be spared "without interruption" for this purpose. The Resident consulted Dr. Bird and forwarded his reply to Government. As a medical authority, his opinion was greatly valued by Government, and I need no apology to quote it here in full. Dr. Bird writes on the 15th of September 1828:—

To,

LIEUTENANT-COLONEL ARCHIBALD ROBERTSON,
RESIDENT, SATARA.

SIR,

I have the honour to acknowledge the receipt of your letter of the 13th instant, together with the copy of one from the Secretary to the Honourable the Governor on the subject of giving my uninterrupted attention to ascertain the nature of the climate of the Mahabaleshwar Hills.

In reference to the paragraph of your letter, requesting me to state how far my medical duties at the Residency might admit of devoting my time to the object, which the Honourable the Governor has in contemplation, I must observe that, though the calls on me by sick members of the Residency are not constant, yet, as the late frequent claims on my attention afford the only means of judging for the future, I could not possibly accomplish the object in view, if a twelve month's residence on the Hills be deemed absolutely necessary. But should the Honourable the Governor think that a residence of one month in each of the periods of the year, namely the hot, rainy and dry seasons, might be sufficient for ascertaining the general nature of the climate, I will be able to give my attention for such a period to this, or even to take charge of the sick from the beginning of February, from which time all the members of the Residency will be in all probability at the Hills.

An accurate register of the thermometer on the Hills for twelve months, with observations on the prevailing winds, and the quantity of rain which may have fallen, is a desideratum regarding the climate, much wanted before any accurate opinion can be formed regarding the propriety of Mahabaleshwar as a convalescent station; but this even is only secondary and of minor importance, to ascertaining what are the effects of the climate on men labouring under disease, when all the benefits of experienced medical treatment have been given them by advantage being taken of that change which the climate at first effects on the constitution; for, without such treatment, a residence on the Hills may be in some cases detrimental. The propriety of Mahabaleshwar as a station for convalescents must ultimately be determined by the result of such an enquiry, and though I would not presume to dicide what is best to be done in such a case; I cannot help observing, that it involves too many interests to be left to the opinion of any one person, however well qualified for his task, and that there would be less chance of ultimate disappointment and failure, provided a Committee of three Medical Officers was appointed to draw up a report of their opinions on the cases that had been treated in hospital, access to them being given for that purpose. The register of the barometer winds, &c., might be kept by an intelligent half-caste writer, for nine months in the year, and the accuracy of such, ascertained by the actual residence of an European on the Hills for the other three months, as I have before suggested.

While I am on this subject, I may be allowed to make one more observation, that the sick man, intended for the change to Mahabaleshwar, should be sent early in the season; as change to any climate, in the commencement of chronic disease after effects a restoration to health, which may be in vain sought for, after a few months longer have been allowed to elapse. On looking over the quarterly returns of disease in two troops of the Horse Artillery for nearly four years, and during which time the men were stationed both in Gujarath and the Deccan, I find that those of them who suffered from chronic affections of the liver after the intermittent and remittent fevers of August, September and October, and who remained in hospital for more than three months, seldom recovered and were generally invalided; but I have great reason to think from what I have seen elsewhere that, had they been sent away for a change of air after medicine had in the first instance failed in its good effects, the result might have then been much more favourable: and if it be ascertained that the Mahabaleshwar hills are quite healthy in October (and of this I doubt not), all chronic cases of two or three months standing, which had been in hospital during the rains, might be sent there with advantage; and whether the result of an enquiry into the nature of the climate be that it is quite inefficient or otherwise in producing a healthy change in the constitution where disease had been long standing, still these Hills, though inferior to the Nilgherries or to England in this respect, may be advantageously resorted to in other cases."

I have the honour to be

SATARA,
15th September 1828.

Sir
Your most obedient servant,
JAMES BIRD,
Surgeon to the Resident at Satara.

In forwarding the above letter to Government, the Resident of Satara made the following remarks:—"Though I was myself doubtful as to our being able conveniently to spare the services of Dr. Bird, who from one cause or another, has frequent calls on his attention, I still deemed it my duty to refer the subject to him, and in doing so, I begged he would at the same time favour me for the consideration of the Honourable the Governor with such observations, as from his knowledge of the climate of the hills he might be of opinion, would prove useful. Dr. Bird's reply I have now the honour to transmit. In laying it before the Honourable the Governor, I beg you will solicit his attention to the offer of Dr. Bird to render himself of use in aiding the sick with his advice at the hills, and also mention that, should his suggestion as to a report from a Committee be honoured with the sanction of the Honourable the Governor, he will be happy to officiate as a member of such Committee." He further added:—"It is Dr. Bird's opinion that the hills will be more likely to prove beneficial to sick persons if they are sent there at as early a stage of their ailings as possible, than after these diseases have become chronic."

It seems that the suggestion made by Dr. Bird for appointing a Committee of

Medical experts at Mahabaleshwar was approved by Government and Surgeon James Walker was appointed to the medical charge of the Convalescent Hospital at Mahabaleshwar, which was established there in October 1828, with a view to observe the effects of the climate on the invalid patients. Dr. Bird was directed to work conjointly with him in addition to his own duties. Drs. Walker and Bird began their special work and communicated the results of their investigation to Government in due course of time. Simultaneously Captain Grafton, a Government Surveyor in the Deccan, was asked to do the survey of the hills. In fact, the beginning was made in right earnest.

His Excellency the Governor, at the request of the Raja, paid a visit to Satara in November 1828. The Raja had made elaborate preparations for the reception of His Excellency. The following account of this grand ceremoney was published by an eye-witness in the "Bombay Courier," and will be found most interesting :—

"On the 6th November, Sir John Malcom's visit to the Maharaja took place on the south bank of the river Yenna about two miles from the place. The *istakbal* was splendid. His Highness, attended by his relations mounted on elephants, with rich trappings, was preceded by 100 peons, and followed by his own native horsemen glittering in green and scarlet. The Governor was preceded by peons and followed by numerous suite, 200 of the Madras Cavalry and Irregular Horse. The Maharaja and the Governor arrived at the same instant, when the embrace of welcome was given, as is usual on such occasions among the Asiatics. The Governor and the Maharaja having then mounted the same elephant, a salute of 21 guns, on the part of the Company, was fired in honour of His Highness; followed by their respective suites, they proceeded through a street formed of the Company's and His Highness's own troops, until within a few hundred yards of the palace, when a salute of nineteen guns was fired on the part of the Rajah, in honour of the Governor. Having soon after alighted, they and the gentlemen present, attended the Darbar, after which the Governor and his suite returned to their encampment. Next day the Maharajah returned the Governor's visit at his tent. In the afternoon he accompanied the latter to the Adawlut, the fine aqueduct lately constructed for supplying the town with water, and the new building called the 'Jal Mandir.' The last is a large room, just a counterpart of the Residency, built for the reception of his European guests. It is situated in a garden, tastefully laid out in small flower-pots, divided by gravel walks, with numerous fountains that keep playing around it on occasions of ceremony. The whole is highly creditable to the Rajah's taste. Here at the Rajah's invitation, on the afternoon of the 12th, nearly sixty gentlemen sat down to dinner; an excellent repast of native dishes, fruits and sweetmeats was served up to them on plates and tables, in the European style; while plenty of generous champagne crowned the banquet with hilarity and warmed the feelings of the guests. Immediately afterwards the Maharajah held a Darbar, and in the evening led his visitors through the town, which was illuminated to see some fireworks at a finely selected spot for this occasion, where the whole of the native population, perched on the surrounding heights, gave an animated beauty to the naturally picturesque appearance of the place."

The impressions made on the Governor by the enthusiastic and cordial reception at Satara were most favourable; and the spirit of improvement and the desire of promoting public good evinced by the Raja on this occasion, gave immense gratification to His Excellency, who, in parting, gave a glowing tribute of praise to the Raja, which he richly deserved. The Raja, in appreciation of the keen personal interest exhibited by the Governor in the establishment of the Mahabaleshwar Sanitarium, agreed to constitute Mahabaleshwar into a separate Pettah (a small taluka) for administrative purposes; and accordingly, on the 23rd December 1828, he forwarded a *yadi* (vernacular letter) with his cousin, Shrimant

Balwant Rao Senapati, to the Resident, Lt.-Col. Robertson, giving his consent to the proposed establishment of a Pettah at Mahabaleshwar. The noble-minded Governor expressed his wish to call the new village after the name of the Raja, in recognition of his valuable services in that cause; but the Raja was most unwilling to accept the honour, as he thought it fit to call the new place after the name of Sir John Malcolm in memory of his visit to Satara and as a token of his sincere regard and friendship. The Raja therefore immediately issued the following proclamation announcing the foundation of Malcolm Peith and inviting traders and merchants to open their shops there.

"Be it known to all the subjects of His Highness Shrimant Maharaja Rajeshri Chhatrapati. There is near Jaoli a mountain on the East of which is the Tai Ghat; on the West near Pratapgad is the Radtondi Ghat; and Coorlsy Ghat, in the South; on the North and in one corner of this mountain is Mahabaleshwar and the source of the holy Krishna. On the summit near this place is a spot, called Nahar (or wilderness), the air of which is remarkably bracing during the hot weather, in consequence of which His Excellency Sir John

Malcolm and English gentlemen have built there houses for themselves and barracks for the soldiers. We likewise intend building on that spot. In order that all necessaries may be at hand, traders should settle on this mountain and form a Pettah there, which certainly will flourish, as trade will be drawn into this channel in consequence of a road which it is our desire to make over the Paur Ghat. Here then, there shall be a Pettah, and it shall be called "Malcolm Peith," and it shall be protected and shall flourish."

The year 1829 was most remarkable as it was a landmark in the history of sanitaria in India by bringing into existence a new and fashionable health-resort. It soon attained great importance and popularity, rising subsequently to the position of a summer capital of the Presidency. It was in the summer of 1829 that Mahabaleshwar was officially declared to be a Sanitarium, and His Excellency the Governor made his own residence there. It may be mentioned here that Sir John Malcolm arrived at Mahabaleshwar early in April with a view to fully enjoy the hot season on the hills. He was accompanied by his Secretary and staff, and a number of friends. During his absence from the seat of Government, Lieut.-General Sir Thomas Bradford was appointed to conduct the administration—all official correspondence continuing to be carried on and the resolutions of Government passed in the name of the Governor-in-Council. This arrangement was specially made in order to remove the inconvenience that was experienced in the past year. The Governor put up at the new bungalow specially built on a beautiful site selected by him. It was named "Mount Charlotte" after his favourite daughter and is now generally known by the name "Mount Malcolm." It possesses a panoramic view which is simply magnificent. The Resident of Satara, Lt.-Col. Robertson, and his Assistant, Mr. William Simson, were present on the hills. The Raja of Satara had come with a large retinue and encamped on his own ground of Raj-mal, where he had built a large and commodious bungalow for himself. This bungalow is not now in existence, but its traces can be seen near the Race Ground, where still exists the Raja's well, known as राजबावडी (Raja's Well). The new station looked gay and lively. The Raja paid his visit to the Governor and received him at his bungalow with great pomp, and entertained him with the musical performance of the well-known musician of his court, Devidas Binkar. The friendly intercourse between the Governor and the Raja promoted mutual good will, confidence and respect, which led to the happy result of firmly establishing the new Sanitarium on these hills, by the exchange of the selected lands with the adjacent village of Paur, to the British Government, for the village of Khandalla near Wai. It is noted in the Raja's diary that, "on the 15th of May 1829, the Raja finally resolved to cede to the British Government the site of Mahabaleshwar selected by Sir John Malcolm and accordingly engaged his word. His Excellency the Governor was exceedingly pleased and said that this act of liberality on the part of the Raja would carry his fame to England, and make the friendship stronger than before between the two Governments." The treaty for this territorial exchange was signed by the Raja on the 16th May 1829 at Mahabaleshwar. It is as follows:—

TREATY.

"Articles of agreement between the Honourable Company on the one part and His Highness the Raja of Satara on the other, regarding a cession by His Highness of certain lands and the village of

Paur on the Mahabaleshwar Hills in the District of Jaolee in exchange for the village of Khandalla in the District of Wai.

1st. The Honourable Company's Government considering it an object of great importance to establish a convalescent depot at Malcolm Peith, situated on the hills contiguous to, and south of, the village of Mahabaleshwar, in the District of Jaolee, and it being necessary, a tract of ground should be ceded for that purpose, both in reference to the expense which must be incurred by the British Government in forming such establishment, as well as to induce others to make such outlays on account of buildings as will render the advantage arising from the climate generally accessible to all who may be desirous of availing themselves thereof, and also for the more effectual control and government of the settlement; His Highness the Raja of Satara hereby makes over in full sovereignty and in perpetuity, to the Honourable Company, the lands adjoining the said Peith or market, called "Malcolm Peith," which are contained within the red line in the map or plan, and the measurement and bearings of which are particularized in the schedule, both of which documents are annexed to this agreement, and the latter of which is denominated a "statement or measurement" of the boundary of the tract attached to "Malcolm Peith," and the convalescent station, on the Mahabaleshar Hill, the whole tract comprizing a space of about 3 square miles, 10 square furlongs, the circumference thereof being 15 miles.

2nd. His Highness further cedes for the same purposes and in order to preclude the likelihood of disputes and misunderstandings between His Highness's Officers and those of the Honourable Company, the Peith and lands of the village of Paur with the exception of the fort of Purtabghar and its established lands; and also such part of the road leading from the boundary of the cession specified in the preceding article to the top of the Paur Ghaut as may not be within the limits of the village of Paur, and a space of two hundred yards English on each side thereof.

3rd. For the better defining of the lands, as well as the line of two hundred yards on each side of the road (as specified in the second article) now ceded by His Highness to the Honourable Company, landmarks will hereafter be put up with the mutual consent of the contracting parties.

4th. In exchange for the above cessions and in consideration of His Highness finishing the road now making to Paur Ghat, the Honourable Company hereby cedes, in full sovereignty, and in perpetuity, to His Highness, the Raja of Satara, the village of Khandalla, situated at the bottom of the Kamatkee Ghaut in the District of Wai, with all the lands, revenues and rights of the Honourable Company in the same.

5th. The Honourable Company engages to levy no duties on the sale or transit of commerce on the line of road, or in the tract of the country now ceded; with the exception of Bazar duties which now are, and have always been levied in the Peith or village of Paur; and His Highness agrees to remove from the top of the Paur Ghaut, his station for collecting duties; establishing the same at such place or places within his own limits, on the interior of the tract now ceded, as may be most convenient."

It may be said to the credit of Sir John Malcolm and the Resident, Lt.-Col. Robertson, that they highly appreciated the valuable and disinterested services of the Raja and brought them to the notice of the higher authorities for recognition and reward. Lt.-Col. Robertson, in forwarding the agreement of the Raja to the Bombay Government, on the 16th May 1829 from Malcolm Peith, justly remarked: "To the Government of Bombay and to the European community of the Presidency, and indeed of the Establishment generally, this road and the cession to which it leads, promise the most important benefits, and while the Honourable the Governor in Council will in this consideration receive more than an adequate recompense for the outlay that has been incurred to the Honourable Company, he will also, I am satisfied, not only fully appreciate the public spirit and liberality of His Highness who with such slender means did so much, but bring his useful and gratifying co-operation in the most favourable manner to the notice of authorities in England, from whom, I would request, that some token of their approbation, worthy of them to give, and of the Raja to receive, should be sent to His Highness." This recommendation was highly approved and supported by the Government of Bombay and duly forwarded on to the Court of Directors in England, who were impressed with a very favourable opinion of the administration of the Raja and desired the Government of Bombay "to signify to the Raja their high satisfaction at his public conduct and his excellent administration." As a mark of distinction they also dispatched on the 29th December 1835 a sword with a letter of testimony to the Government of Bombay to be presented to the Raja. But through a curious irony of fate, the Raja afterwards came under the displeasure of the Bombay Government, and both the letter and the sword remained in the possession of the Government at Bombay.*

* The letter addressed by the Court of Directors to the Raja of Satara on the 29th December 1835 was afterwards published in the Parliamentary Papers on the Satara Raja. It is as follows :—

"Your Highness,"

"We have been highly gratified by the information from time to time transmitted to us by our Government on the subject of Your Highness's exemplary fulfilment of the duties of that elevated situation in which it has pleased Providence to place you.

The Raja of Satara, who was justly proud of the part taken by him in this affair and much more of his friendship with the Governor, wrote the following account of these transactions to his old friend Captain Grant Duff on the 18th July 1829:—"Mahabaleshwar with its vicinity, in a direct line, as far as the Paur Ghaut, including the village within its range, has been chosen on account of its good climate; and in exchange thereto, it was settled that Khandalla, situated on the Poona Road, should be given to this Government (*i.e.* the Raja of Satara). The climate of this quarter was well approved of by all the

---

"A course of conduct so suitable to Your Highness's exalted station, and so well calculated to promote the prosperity of your dominions and the happiness of your people, as that which you have wisely and uniformly persued, while it reflects the highest honour on your character, has imparted to our minds the feelings of unqualified satisfaction and pleasure. The liberality also which you have displayed in executing at your own cost various public works of great utility and which has so justly raised your reputation in the eyes of the princes and people of India, gives you an additional claim to our approbation, respect, and applause.

"Impressed with these sentiments, the Court of Directors of the East India Company have unanimously resolved to transmit to you a sword, which will be presented to you through the Government of Bombay, and which we trust you will receive with satisfaction as a token of their high esteem and regard.

"With sincere wishes for your health and prosperity, we subscribe ourselves, in the name of the Court."

Your Highness's most faithful friends,

W. S. CLARKE, Chairman,

J. R. CARNAC, Deputy Chairman.

European Gentlemen, as best calculated for the preservation of their health. Here are Government Bungalows. This spot is situated on the way to Pratapghar from Satara. From the latter place a road of 20 kosse in length, leading up to Paur Ghaut, has been made by this Government, and Sir John is making the road on the other side of that Ghaut as far as Mahr (Mahad). He has honoured us here at Satara with a visit, and his reception took place with great ceremony and festivity; and at this happy juncture, when a quite new water-mansion (like a summer house surrounded by fountains on the very brink of a tank) was just erected by us, the articles of glass you had sent from England have arrived here and served very well for its use and decoration. The present Governor is distinguished for the information he possesses of this Court, his taking pains personally in pleasing others, and for his cordiality and magnanimity. It is difficult, we think, to see again a Governor of this stamp."*

---

* Extract from the copy of the Raja's English letter to Captain Grant Duff; dated the 18th July 1829.

CHAPTER IV.

THE NEW SANITARIUM.

Its growth.

NOTHING is more interesting than the study of the rise and progress of the Mahabaleshwar hill station which has been enjoying almost unbroken prosperity since its establishment in 1829. Owing to the encouragement and support of Government, it rose gradually in extent, importance and popularity; and now it is pre-eminently classed as the first and best Sanitarium in Western India, being visited by a large number of people requiring change for the benefit of their health. Besides its fine climate, it affords numerous facilities and comforts, scarcely found at any other hill station. This remarkable progress in its development is solely due to the early efforts of its founders. It is therefore intended to take a bird's-eye view of their work during the early period.

Sir John Malcolm, the founder of the Mahabaleshwar Sanitarium, made his first residence there in 1829, and again visited the place in the hot season of 1830. This being his last visit to these charming hills, he devoted his full attention to carrying out his plans as vigorously and rapidly as he could. The public buildings that were under construction, became now ready for the use of European officers and soldiers. These consisted chiefly of a 'Sanitarium' containing eight sets of quarters and five detached bungalows for the accommodation of sick officers and their families, exclusive of the Doctor's quarters and the hospital. They are still in existence in an altered form. The blocks of the 'Sanitarium' that have since been converted into 'Club Chambers' can now be identified near the Frere Hall. The bungalows which were once mere thatched cottages are at present known as the Government Bungalows. They were built at long distances in the valley known as 'Clifton Valley,'—so named after the native place of Sir C. J. Napier. The hospital, which was destroyed by fire two or three times, is still in its own place near the Club Chambers, but is now destined to be removed to a better situation. The Doctor's bungalow, known for a long time as 'Walker Sab kâ Bungalow' is the present 'Woodside,' the permanent residence of the Superintendent of Mahabaleshwar. Dr. Walker, the first Medical Officer of the Convalescent Station established on the Mahabaleshwar hills, was placed in charge of these buildings and allotment of quarters at the station by a Government order dated the 20th February 1829; and for his guidance certain rules were framed and passed by them on the 22nd November 1829. Under the observation of the Medical Officer there was kept a detachment of 40 sepoys, and Ensign J. W. Auld, 26th N. I., was ordered to command native details employed at the Convalescent Station. The result of the experiment of the year 1829 was most satisfactory, and the following remarks of Dr. Walker, who wrote under the nom de plume "Resident of Malcolm Peith," are most interesting:—

"The warm season is now over, and experience has proved that in a good house there is not one day in the whole year that can be deemed hot at this mountain-residence. The wind, blow from what quarter it will, is always cool, and throughout the whole year, a blanket is always required at night. The four months of the monsoon are yet to be tried by Europeans; but I am satisfied, from the health of a detachment of 40 sepoys who remained in the past season, that notwithstanding the fogs in which the mountain is often enveloped, and the frequent, though not heavy, rain which is said to fall, the station is not unhealthy during these months. From the testimony of the inhabitants cholera is unknown, and fevers are very rare, while the experience we have yet had, both of Europeans and their native followers, confirms this fact. The convalescent soldiers have, I believe, improved much this year, though several hopeless cases were sent and arrived only to die, which is to be regretted, as this climate, though it may effect wonders, cannot be expected to work miracles. Amongst the gentlemen who repaired here for their health, all have benefited and some in a degree quite surprising."

"Considering the short distance from Bombay, which can during nine months of the year be reached in 24 hours and is an easy journey of two days, I must believe that we shall early have plenty of good houses to rent. There cannot be a doubt that the first speculations in building will prove very profitable; and it is to be desired they should, and that to those who aid in promoting its object of rendering these hills the resort of invalids, the Government should give the most liberal encouragement."

"Among the many improvements at this station, none promises to be more beneficial than a large garden, which Mr. Smith, a most intelligent and energetic Indo-Britain in the service of the Raja of Sattara, has been aided by the Government to form. A large well has been sunk and built up with masonry, which will irrigate three or four acres of excellent soil, that is already prepared to receive the abundant supplies of seeds and plants which are to be furnished from Dhapooree. Dr. Lush, the Superintendent of the Company's Botanical Garden, recently visited us, and approved of the spot selected for the first horticultural experiments at this station, where, there is every reason to hope, we shall be able to cultivate with success European fruits as well as all the vegetables already introduced into India."

"Besides the advantages which Mahabaleshwar possesses in climate and position, it has great recommendations in the beauty of its scenery. This will have a salutary influence upon invalids and must, now that the approach is facilitated by excellent roads down the Western Ghauts, render it a place of resort to visitors, whose temporary residence will promote its cheerfulness, and add, by the demand created, to its market and other conveniences as a convalescent station."

These remarks of Dr. Walker bear ample testimony to the progress achieved in the development of the Sanitarium in the first year of its establishment. It involved heavy expenditure on the part of Government in its preliminary stages, though it promised great advantages in the future. The spirit of enterprise, earnestness of purpose, and devoted love for the cause, were the characteristic qualities of Sir John Malcolm that ensured the success of his exertions, and the Sanitarium eventually became a very popular and beneficial institution, and fully satisfied the expectations of its founders and promoters. On the 1st June 1830, the Raja of Satara wrote from Malcolm Peith to his friend Captain Grant Duff:—"Sir John Malcolm, the Governor, has rapidly improved Malcolm Peith and brought it to a flourishing state." *

* In the same year Dr. Murray, Superintendent of Mahabaleshwar, paid the following tribute of praise to Sir John Malcom:—"The advantages thus offered might long have remained unappreciated and neglected, or known only to a few in their immediate neighbourhood, had not the attention of Sir John Malcolm been fortunately directed to this subject, and an early visit enabled him to form a just estimate of the qualities of the climate. To his unwearied support and ardent promotion of every measure calculated to establish and improve the station, is this Presidency indebted for the benefits it has reaped, and will continue to reap, from this source."

Such a striking success was sufficient to impress a nature like that of Sir John Malcolm, and the natural charms of the place gladdened his heart so much that he wrote from Malcolm Peith on the 15th May 1830 to express his feelings to his friend, Sir Walter Scott :—"I must, if not born an enthusiast, be rendered one by my present position. I write by the light of a window through which, from an elevation of 4,700 feet, I have a fine view of the sea looking over what these, 3000 feet below, call high mountains; the air in this hottest of our months is such as to give a spring to both body and soul, and were it not for my occupation and absence from those I love, I could be content to dwell amid such scenes as those by which I am surrounded, for the remainder of my existence."

Sir John Malcolm relinquished his exalted office on the 1st of December 1830 and was succeeded by the new Commander-in-Chief, Sir Sidney Beckwith, as Governor of Bombay. In his parting minute on the administration of the Bombay Presidency, Sir John referred to the progress of his favourite Sanitarium, Malcolm Peith, on the 30th November 1830, in the following terms : "This station has more than realised my expectation. The extraordinary salubrity of Malcolm Peith and its beneficial effects in the preservation and restoration of health have been fully attested to by an experience of two years, and should a permanent military station be formed at this place or its immediate vicinity where the monsoon is less severe, I feel confident that it will be the means of saving health and lives of hundreds of Europeans."

Sir John Malcolm left Bombay on the 5th December 1830, leaving behind him his illustrious name ever shining on the salubrious hills of Mahabaleshwar. Another monument which still keeps his memory green is his noble statue in marble by Chantrey. It adorns the Town Hall of Bombay.

The next decade from 1831 to 1840 was one of prosperity and advancement to Malcolm Peith. It, however, experienced a sad catastrophe in the first month of its commencement in the death of the new Governor, Sir Sidney Beckwith, who passed away suddenly on these hills, on the 15th January 1831. His remains are buried under a monolith which forms a worthy monument erected on these hills in testimony of the admiration for his noble character by a small circle of his friends. After the death of Sir Sidney Beckwith, Honourable the Earl of Clare was appointed Governor of Bombay, who visited these hills every year and took considerable interest in their welfare. With the Governor there was also a noticeable change of the Medical Officer of the station. Dr. James Walker, who had expended so much energy and labour in improving the Sanitarium, was promoted to the Medical Store Department of the Presidency on the 26th March 1831; and Assistant Surgeon James Murray was appointed to assume the charge of the Convalescent Station on the Mahabaleshwar hills.

Dr. Murray's name is familiar at Mahabaleshwar even to this day. "The Murray Peith" and "The Murray House" are still well-known there. He was associated with the affairs of Mahabaleshwar hills for a long time. Later on, he was connected with the Satara Residency, still keeping up his interest in the station, and was a constant visitor of Malcolm Peith.* He

---

* Dr. Murray retired in the early sixties and died at Melrose. An esteemed friend of Dr. Murray has paid the following tribute to his memory in 1863:—

"Dr. Murray was one of the ablest of the many able men that have advanced the Indian Medical Service; although from his retiring disposition, his extensive attainments, profound ability, and great practical sagacity, were fully known and appreciated only by those who enjoyed the privilege of his private friendship. None knew and valued him more, both as a man and a medical officer, than our present Governor (Sir Bartle Frere) and his excellent lady. His studious habits had seriously injured his constitution before he went home, and he enjoyed only a brief period, in a pleasant retreat near Melrose, the rest and retirement he had so well earned."

first attracted the notice of the late Governor, Sir John Malcolm, by his talents, ability and tact; and was on the 1st November 1828 nominated to the medical charge of the detachment of the 17th Madras Light Infantry, which then formed the Governor's escort. He served on the Governor's personal staff from 1828 to 1830, and was appointed the Superintendent of Malcolm Peith in 1831. He made the hill station very popular and attractive by constructing new roads and opening up several views such as "Elphinstone Point," "Sidney Point," and naming them after the illustrious Governors. The first name celebrated here was that of Elphinstone, the great statesman and conciliator of Maharashtra. The second was that of Sir Sidney Beckwith, whose memory was then fresh owing to his sad death on these hills. Dr. Murray also built a small rest-house, merely a cottage, on the promontory of the Elphinstone Point in order that the visitors might enjoy the most sublime and picturesque scenery there. This old cottage has now been converted into a decent bungalow, still bearing the name 'Murray Mahal.'

The following description of the flourishing condition of Mahabaleshwar given by Dr. Murray in 1836 throws much light on the progress made in the first eight years:—"Although only eight years have elapsed since the establishment of this station, the hills are already intersected by excellent roads in every direction, for which we are indebted partly to the liberality of the Raja of Sattara, but principally to the munificent contribution of the numerous visitors who have during this period resorted to the station. These roads, which now extend over a space exceeding forty miles, while they afford to the invalid the means of varying and prolonging his rides, open up to him at every point, a varied succession of mountain scenery, which for grandeur and beauty is scarcely to be equalled in any part of the world, and which constitutes by no means the least attractive feature of the station. The more than Alpine grandeur of the scenery around Elphinstone and Sydney Points, the picturesque fall of the Yenna, and the exquisite beauty of prospect from the several headlands which overlook the Tamb valley, will at once occur to the memory of every one who has had an opportunity of visiting them."

During the above mentioned period there was a marked increase in the number of visitors, which also proves the popularity of this hill station. The following statement shows the number of visitors of all ages, who had resorted to Mahabaleshwar each season, from the year 1831-32 to 1839-40 :—

Year.	Number of visitors.
1831-32	197
1832-33	168
1833-34	209
1834-35	210
1835-36	240
1836-37	252
1837-38	313
1838-39	265
1839-40	307

It must be borne in mind that there was no Railway communication between Mahabaleshwar and Bombay, and even the cart traffic was almost unknown in those days. The visitor had to ride a horse or be carried in a palanquin by professional coolies, called dooly-bearers. During this period Mahabaleshwar was made accessible both from Bombay and from the principal stations of the Deccan. The visitor from Bombay by sailing down the coast to Bankote, and thence up the river Savitri to Mahad (a distance of seventy miles by sea, and thirty by river) was brought within twenty-seven miles land journey from the hills. The distance from Poona by an indifferent hilly route was seventy miles, and from Satara only thirty miles by a very good carriage road, which was completed by the Raja in 1830.

It is not possible to get the census figures of Mahabaleshwar of this period which could have given a correct idea of the whole population. But from the information available, it appears that in 1840 there were only 70 private dwelling houses, of which 53 were substantially built of hewn stone and lime, and the remainder of rough stone and mortar, sun-dried bricks or wattle-work. The greater number of them were thatched, tiles having been found not to resist the monsoon rain. Allotments of ground for building purposes were granted by Government on a twenty-one years' lease, the principal provisions of which were that the lessee was to pay an annual rent at the rate of a rupee an acre and to build a substantial bungalow and erect suitable landmarks on the boundaries of his allotment. The average size of individual allotments granted during the years 1838, 1839 and 1840 was six acres.

As regards the trade there were six European shops, where European supplies of almost every description were procurable at the same rate as at Poona and a little higher than at Bombay. The itinerant hawkers (Bhoras) from Bombay used to visit the station annually with baskets full of varied goods, both European and Indian. The Malcolm Peith Bazar, which only now retains the name of 'Malcolm Peith,' was a tolerably large one, and was well supplied with all articles of daily consumption. The European establishment consisted only of a Chaplain and a Medical Officer. The former visited Dapoli once a month and Ratnagiri once in two months during the fair season, and during the rains he performed the duties of a Chaplain at Malegaum. The Medical Officer was both Superintendent of the station and First Assistant to the Magistrate, and had charge of a treasure chest for the payment of sick officers and their families. A detachment of 50 sepoys under the command of a jamadar was kept up to supply the usual guard. In addition to these, a subsidiary jail, containing 60 Chinese convicts who were employed in the construction and repair of roads, a chowdi (now turned into Mahalkari's Office) and a dharmashala for native travellers were also opened. The Chinese convicts introduced the cultivation of potatoes of excellent qualities on these hills in 1832; and it is mostly owing to their industry that potatoes and English vegetables yielded an abundant supply not only to the station but to Poona and Bombay markets also. It was Mr. B. Hutt, (Bombay Civil Service) Assistant Judge at Thana, who suggested in 1830 the sending of a body of Chinese convicts to the Mahabaleshwar hills as a reformatory experiment, which proved in every way a most complete success, and to which we owe the successful introduction of the culture of the potato, which has since become one of the staple products of Western India.*

Amongst the visitors the largest number was that of Europeans, mostly high officers of Government, Civil and Military. The Resident of Satara was a conspicuous figure playing an important part in the social life of the station. Lt.-Col. Robertson had his own bungalow on the Sindola Hill, which was known for many years as the "Sindola Park" or the Residency Bungalow, and is now the property of the Chief of Miraj (Senior). At its entrance on the western side, near the

---

* For more information about Chinese Convicts on the Mahabaleshwar Hills, see Appendix.

"Four Oaks," there is an unnoticed grave of his two dearly loved children, Matilda and Colin Campbell, who died on these hills in 1829 and 1830. Lt.-Col. Robertson retired in January 1832, and was succeeded by Lt.-Col. Peter Lodwick as the Resident at Satara. This is the same gentlaman who first brought these hills to the notice of the public in 1824. He had great liking for this place and utilised every opportunity for its betterment.

The first European marriage that was celebrated here was that of Captain T. B. Jervis, the renowned scholar and mathematician, with Anne Sarah, youngest daughter of the late Dr. William Paget of Exmouth, Devonshire, on the 15th November 1830.

The Raja of Satara who contributed immensely to the establishment of this hill station, continued his interest in it till 1837. It appears from his diary that he did not fail to pay his visits to the hills in the hot season almost every year. It was his intention to build a large lake on the hills for the public use, and got its estimate prepared by his own Engineer, Ranoji Naik; but he could not spare a large sum of money as the project was too costly. It is mentioned in his diary that, "on the 23rd

May 1836, Lt.-Col. Lodwick estimated the cost upto Rs. 10,000; but the Raja said that it would not suffice even to make a mud wall. He therefore proposed that he would pay the sum in cash and the lake may be built by him (the Resident). The delay in this matter was due to other demands on the Raja's purse, chiefly the marriage of his brother, which cost him Rs. 40,000."

Lt.-Col. Lodwick and the Raja were on friendly terms; the former never departed from the respectful line of conduct he had always observed towards His Highness. But about the year 1837, the stars of the Raja changed, and some political differences arose between him and the Government of Bombay, which led to the deposition of the Raja from the throne. The history of his case is still a mystery. The deposed Raja was sent to Benaras and a pension of Rs. 1,20,000 was given to him and his family. On his behalf some attempts were made in England by his agents and sympathisers to appeal to the Court of Directors, but they all proved unsuccessful. It is significant, however, to note that all the Residents from Grant Duff to Lodwick supported the deposed Raja and stood by his side.

The exiled Raja died at Benaras on the 14th October 1847.

It was a most unfortunate coincidence that the evil influence of the Raja's stars reflected on those of the Resident, Lt.-Col. Lodwick, who was also removed from Satara in 1837 and offered the temporary appointment of Quarter-Master General of the Army, which he declined in consequence of ill health, and proceeded to Europe on sick leave. It is strange that both these zealous promoters of the Mahabaleshwar Sanitarium—the Raja of Satara and his Resident—should suffer the bad effects of their stars simultaneously. General Lodwick died in France in 1873 at the advanced age of 90 years.

In the misfortune of the Raja, Mahabaleshwar had also a share inasmuch as it lost a fine building. The Raja, when he saw that the wind was blowing against him, in a fit of dispair, ordered his bungalow to be demolished. It is noted in his diary that, "on the 30th April 1837, he made up his mind to demolish the bungalow at Mahabaleshwar, as his relations with the British Government were far from satisfactory. The Resident, Col. Lodwick, and another Military Officer, a Col. Blake (?), advised him not to do so. But the Raja said:

"when there will be साफी (restoration of friendly relations between the two Governments), a new bungalow can be erected in no time." Such was the sad end of the Raja's bungalow at Mahabaleshwar!

At this time Sir James Rivett Carnac was the Governor of Bombay, who succeeded Sir Robert Grant on the 31st May 1839. He visited Mahabaleshwar in October 1839 after issuing his famous proclamation for removing the Raja Pratap Sing from the *gadi* and placing his brother Shahaji alias Appa Saheb on it.* From Mahabaleshwar he specially went down to Satara to perform the installation ceremony of the new Raja, which took place on the 18th November 1839. On this occasion, His Excellency the Governor took an opportunity to put forth the claims of Mahabaleshwar on the

---

* The following extract from his letter dated Mahabaleshwar, 23rd November 1839, gives the account of his eventful visit to Satara:—

"I left this (Mahabaleshwar) on the 16th to attend the inauguration of the Raja of Satara, from which place I returned last night. The affair went off admirably in all respects. There was a great show and parade on the occasion and during the various subsequent ceremonies. I took the opportunity of this visit to suggest to the Raja, the institution of a College at Satara and the establishment of village Schools—also an hospital, and the improvement of roads and construction of bridges, all of which he will do. He cannot dispose of his surplus revenue and of the funds in his treasury to better advantage than for purposes of general advantage in his own dominions—he will soon change the face of it by the improvements he has in contemplation, and in which he apperas to take great interest."

—*Calcutta Review*, Vol. CXXIX, page 344.

Mahabaleshwar Lake.

benevolence of the new Raja of Satara, while suggesting to him several works of general improvement and utility. The Raja accepted the suggestion most willingly, and undertook to build a tank at Mahabaleshwar. On his return, H. E. the Governor consulted Dr. Murray, the Superintendent of the Convalescent Station at Mahabaleshwar, on the subject, who gave his opinion that, "the construction of this bund will be extremely beneficial to the station both by improving the qualities of the climate and by affording an increased supply of water for the purposes of cultivation and of domestic use."*

---

* Letter from Dr. J. Murray to J. P. Willoughby, Esq., Secretary in attendance on the Hon'ble the Governor, dated Malcolm Peith, 30th November 1839. In this letter Dr. Murray makes the following further remarks :—

"The principal objection which has been urged against this climate is the feeling of dryness and constriction of skin which it produces during certain months. Although this is to a certain extent, the resnlt of the rarefication of the atmosphere, and is more or less characteristic of all elevated regions, yet it is in part also produced by the dryness of the air and is consequently most felt during those months when there is least atmospheric moisture. It is obvious, therefore, that the continued evaporation from a large body of water by diffusing an additional quantity of aqueous vapour in the atmosphere would go a considerable way towards remedying the inconvenience now referred to. Thus the formation of a lake, such as that now proposed, would tend materially to improve the agreeable qualities of the climate ; while the elevation of the Station and the rocky natnre of the ground (which notwithstanding the enormons fall of rain during the monsoon never presents a muddy or swampy appearance) forbid any apprehension being entertained of malaria and its attendant diseases.

The Governor, thereupon, intimated to the Raja his high gratification for his laudable undertaking and asked him to take further steps to carry it out. Mr. Smith, Civil Engineer, in the service of the Raja of Satara, was entrusted with the construction of the new lake, which was completed in 1842. The active interest, thus shown by Sir James Rivett Carnac, in securing for Mahabaleshwar an extensive artificial lake that materially added to the supply of water and gave beauty to the place, made his name popular on these hills, and the "Carnac Point" was gracefully named after him.* It will thus appear that the progress achieved in the first ten years in developing the Sanitarium in various ways was highly satisfactory.

"The benefits which would arise from the construction of the bund, as affording the means of yielding at all times an abundant supply of water, both for domestic use and for the purpose of cultivation, are so obvious as not to require further remarks. But I would like to notice one advantage which may arise from it, of no inconsiderable importance, though, perhaps, small in comparison with others; I allude to the facility it would afford for watering some of the principal roads, the dustiness of which, during the hot season, has long been a source of much incovenience and discomfort.

"Altogether I am of opinion that the formation of this lake will be one of the most important boons which His Highness the Raja of Satara could confer upon the European and Native Society of this Station."

* Sir James Rivett Carnac was one of the most popular and able Governors who ruled over the Bombay Presidency in the 19th century. Mr. A. L. Anderson, C.S., in a public meeting held in Bombay on the 28th April 1841, paid the following tribute of praise to this famous personage:—

The next ten years from 1841 to 1850 witnessed many changes in the political atmosphere of the Deccan, the most important being the death of the last Raja of Satara on the 5th April 1848, and the annexation of his State to the British dominions in consequence of the failure of rightful heir to the Satara throne. This brought the Mahabaleshwar hills under the direct control of the British Government. The last Raja of Satara, who was loyal and benevolent, made his career famous by many works of public utility. The Resident at his Court was Colonel Ovans, who succeeded Lt.-Col. Lodwick in 1837. He visited Mahabaleshwar annually; but most of his time was taken up by the political duties at Satara which were rather of a delicate nature owing to a change in the administration. His successor was Major James Outram, who took up the appointment of Resident and Commandant of the Troops at Satara on the 20th May 1845. He was a great admirer of the Mahabaleshwar hills and wrote his famous book "the Persian Campaign"

"By his unaffected kindness of demeanour, by his unostentatious virtues, by the open heart and by the liberal hand—he so endeared himself to all, that his name will ever be familiar as a household word upon our lips and his memory will be deeply graven on the fleshy tablets of our heart."

there. He was transferred to Baroda in May 1847, when he was enjoying the cool climate of Mahabaleshwar with his wife. He parted with great regret from this place as it seems from his letter to his mother, dated 17th May 1847, in which he writes :—"All well and quite reconciled to the change, though we certainly shall look back to these hills with regret." He was followed by Mr. Bartle Frere, (afterwards Sir Bartle Frere), whose name is cherished at Mahabaleshwar and Satara.

The well-known Governor of the period was Sir George Arthur, who succeeded Sir James Rivett Carnac on the 9th June 1841, and ruled over the destinies of Bombay till the 5th August 1846. His name was held in great respect at Mahabaleshwar owing to his several useful acts and has been associated with its prosperity from generation to generation. The most beautiful point on the Mahabaleshwar hills, still known by his name "Arthur's Seat," was his favourite place of resort, whence he saw into the depths below the majesty of nature—the art of God. The interest of the Arthurs in Mahabaleshwar has been maintained to this day. The son and the grandson of Sir George Arthur held charge of this station for several years as Collector of the Satara District.

View of Arthur's Seat, Mahabaleshwar.

It is not contemplated here to touch the events of the succeeding period even briefly, as they belong to more modern times and are quite fresh in the memory of several people. Yet it will not be well to close the chapter without mentioning one or two important facts in connection with its later progress. Mahabaleshwar owes its present prosperity greatly to the strenuous efforts of Sir Bartle Frere, who, first as Resident of Satara, and after the lapse of the Satara State to the British Government as Commissioner of the District (1849-50), and then as Governor of the Presidency (1862-67), materially assisted to raise its importance and popularity to a great extent. His genial nature and sympathy for the natives, and especially, great regard for the aristocracy of the Deccan, earned for him great reputation and popularity. "At Satara," writes the late Mr. Justice Ranade in 1870, "his native nobility of manners, openness of heart and his chivalrous tenderness for fallen greatness, found their proper field......... Sir Bartle Frere's residence at Satara brought him into intimate contact with the best characteristics of native society, and he there formed his lasting acquaintances with his numerous friends among the native aristocracy. The country of Maharashtra with its hill forts, its picturesque ghauts, and their wild scenery, its brilliant history and its valorous people, there he loved."* On account of these striking qualifications of Sir Bartle Frere, many Indian Princes, Sardars, nobles and men of light and leading, were attracted to the Mahabaleshwar hills in the early sixties and were induced to reside there. The Chiefs of Phaltan, Bhor, Aundh and Jath and those of the S. M. C. States, and leading men of Bombay like Dr. Bhau Daji, Raosaheb Mandlik, Balaji Pandurang, Murarji Gokuldas, Dinshaw Manockjee Pettit, Sir Jamsetjee Jejeebhoy, Cowasji Shapoorjee, Framji Nusserwanjee, Dorabjee Pestonjee, David Sassoon, Nawab Jaffer Ali Khan and many others became constant visitors of Mahabaleshwar in his time, and several of them own properties on the hills. This annual exodus of Indian Sardars and gentlemen materially helped to increase the prosperity of the station. The name of Sir Bartle Frere was perpetuated in 1865 by the erection of the Frere Hall by public subscription in a central position at Mahabaleshwar, which forms a worthy monument to his

* Introduction to the speeches and writings of Sir Bartle Frere by late Mr. M. G. Ranade.

FRERE HALL, MAHABALESHWAR.

noble qualities that permanently won the affection and esteem of the people of this Presidency.

The further progress of the growth of Mahabaleshwar is a matter of pride and satisfaction to those who have taken a keen interest in its welfare. It will form the subject of quite a separate chapter. The immense increase in the number of bungalows that have since sprung up (from 7 in 1840 to 200 in 1915); the gradual extension of several beautiful roads, pleasant bridle-paths, rides; the welcome adjuncts of civilized life—clubs, hotels and gymkhanas for Europeans, Hindus and Parsees, for amusement and recreation; the agreeable additions of Polo ground, Race and Golf courses &c; the erection of charitable institutions such as the Hindu Sanatorium and the Willingdon Hospital and others, all have materially added to the development of the station and largely contributed to the comfort and pleasure of visitors. The Post and the Telegraph, the first heralds of modern civilization, have combined together to fulfil the wants of the public more efficiently and quickly, and have been enjoying the first and uppermost place on these hills. The happy advent of the swift automobile has removed all the fatigue and trouble of the journey and made it quite easy and comfortable. Electricity was only awaiting its chance; and through the kindness of our present popular Governor and his amiable and philanthropic consort, it was allowed to put in its dazzling appearance in the Government House at Mahabaleshwar in April 1915. There is every hope that the whole station will be "electrified" in the near future. In achieving this marvellous success, many distinguished personages have devoted their energy and attention, and their names have been gratefully commemorated on these hills. It is hoped that the same interest in the prosperity of these hills, that still reflects brilliant lustre on its early founders, both Indians and Europeans, will continue to be taken; and the happy and cordial relations of friendship and good will, will be promoted amongst all classes, who meet together on these beautiful hills for a common purpose.

GOVERNMENT HOUSE, MAHABALESHWAR.

MAP OF M

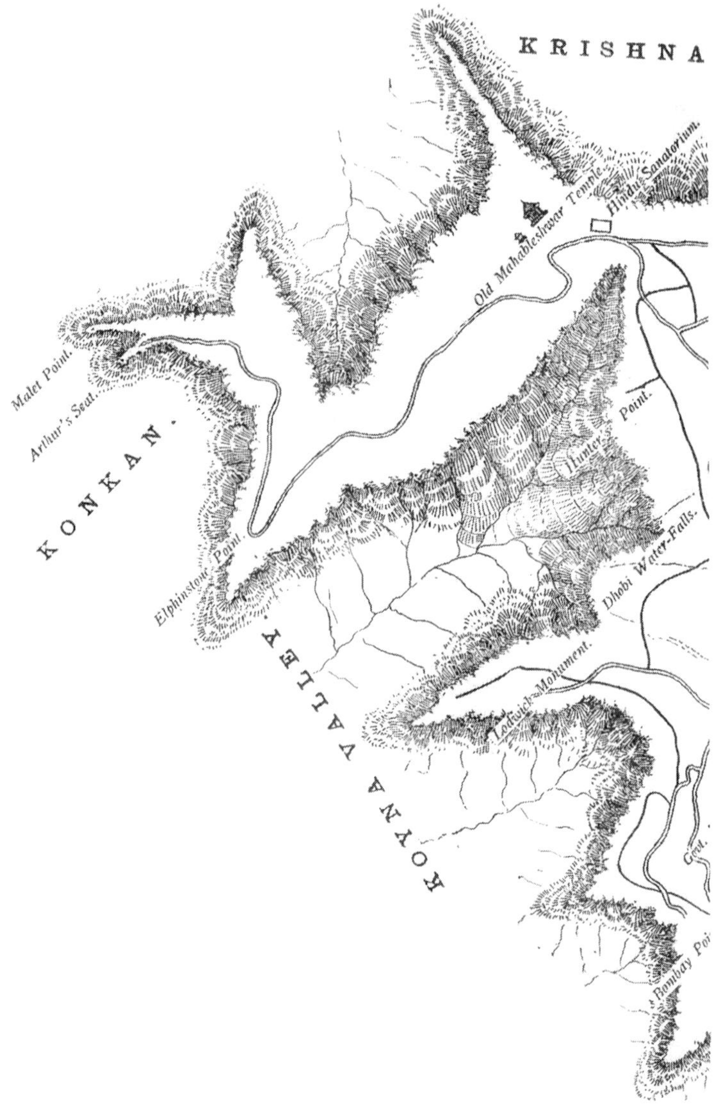

KRISHNA
Hindu Sanatorium.
Old Mahableshwar Temple.
Malet Point.
Arthur's Seat.
KONKAN.
Elphinstone Point.
KOYNA VALLEY.
Hunter's Point.
Dhobi Water-Falls.
Lodwick Monument.
Bombay Poi

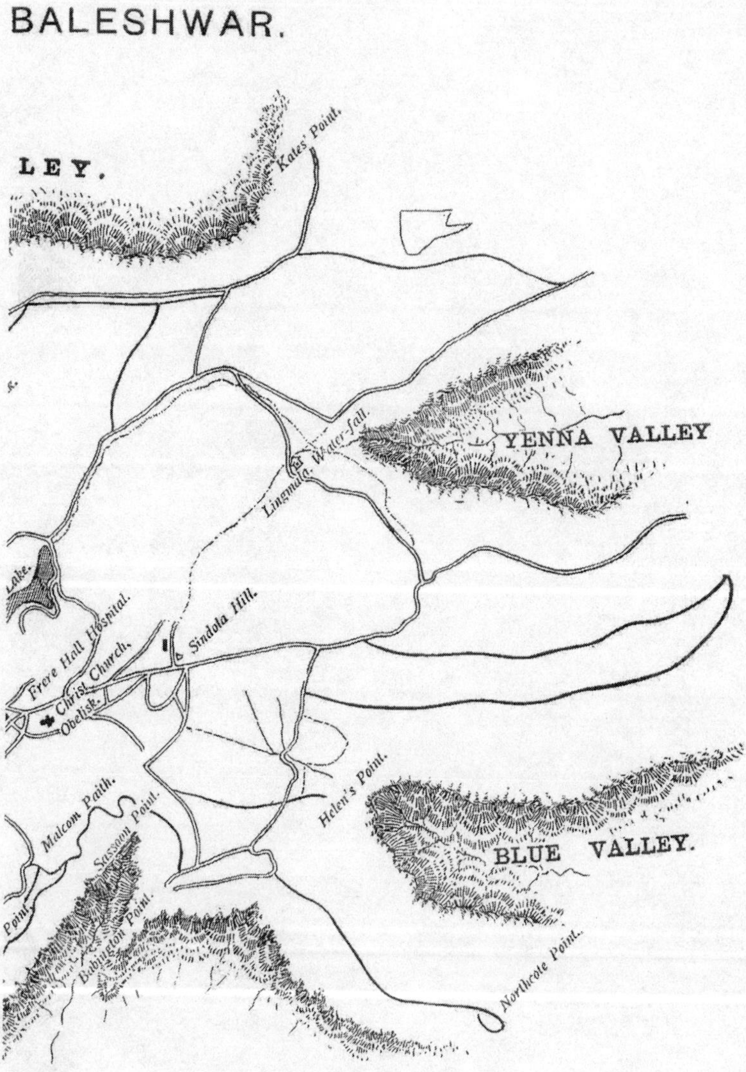
BALESHWAR.
LEY.
Kates' Point.
YENNA VALLEY
Lingmala Water-fall.
Lake.
Frere Hall Hospital.
Christ Church.
Obelisk.
Sindola Hill.
Helen's Point.
Malcom Paith.
Sassoon Point.
Point.
Babington Point.
BLUE VALLEY.
Northcote Point.
OYNA VALLEY.

CHAPTER V.

PLACES OF INTEREST.

I. The Beckwith Monument.

THE Beckwith Monument stands on a commanding position at Mahabaleshwar about 60 yards west to the Church. It is 4,558 feet above sea-level and is visible from all the neighbouring hills. It is a plain obelisk, about 30 feet high, raised in memory of H. E. Lieut.-General Sir T. Sidney Beckwith, K.C.B., Commander-in-Chief of the Bombay Army and Provisional Governor of Bombay, who succeeded Sir John Malcolm, the founder of the Mahabaleshwar Sanitarium, on the 1st December A.D. 1830. Immediately after the charge of Governorship was taken, Sir Sidney Beckwith went to Mahabaleshwar with his Private Secretary, Major Thomas Powell, to recoup his health, but died there suddenly on the 15th of January 1831, at 12 A.M. His remains were buried here on a higher summit of the hill amidst wild scenery. After his death, the office of the Governor was assumed by the Hon'ble John

Romer, the senior Member of Council, who announced the sad event by a special proclamation on the 17th January 1831. The Hon'ble John Romer, Major-General James Stephenson, C.B., the Acting Commander-in-Chief, and other friends of the departed Governor, erected in his memory the present monument by private subscription (Rs. 3,000) and put the following inscription upon it:—

"Sacred to the Memory of
Lieutenant-General Sir Thomas Sidney Beckwith,
K.C.B., Governor and Commander-in-Chief of Bombay
and Colonel of His Majesty's Rifle Brigade;
who, after a long course of distinguished service,
expired at his Residence on these Hills, on the
15th day of January 1831,
aged 60 years.

Erected by a small circle of his friends in testimony of their admiration for his noble character, and to perpetuate the memory of so good and amiable a man."

Lady Beckwith sent another marble tablet to be placed on the Memorial which contains the following touching words:—

"This Tablet is placed by Mary, Lady Beckwith, daughter of the late Sir William Douglas, of Kilhead, Bart., as a memorial of the most devoted affection for her lamented husband, by whose sudden death she has been deprived of a most attached partner and friend and guide, in whom was combined every amiable quality by which the Christian character is adorned, and the intercourse of domestic life is endeared—a loss which can only be alleviated by the hope that looks beyond the grave. The sympathizing friends who erected this monument have kindly permitted a sorrowing widow to add her heartfelt tribute to theirs."

Sir Sidney Beckwith was a great man of his days, and his loss was deeply felt by the Presidency. The "Bombay Courier" published the following obituary notice on Sir Sidney Beckwith :—

"To recount the private virtues of the late Sir Sidney Beckwith would be needless, as the society of this Presidency has had ample opportunity of knowing and appreciating his mild, considerate, and gentlemanly bearing. In the words of one of our living poets he may be said to have ever been :—

> "True as his own sword,
> Of admirable temper, clear and bright,
> Polished and keen, though pliant yet upright."

"The public acts of the late Sir Sidney Beckwith's life are to be found in the campaigns of the late Lord Cornwallis in India, and in the history of the Rifle Brigade in Europe, of which he has well been styled "the father." Sir Sidney Beckwith first entered the army in the 71st Regiment, then serving in India, with which he continued several years, and with it returned to Europe.

"Whilst employed in India, he formed a friendship with Sir John Malcolm, one of his earliest companions in arms, and with whom he was associated almost to the last moments of his life.

"On the return of Sir Sidney Beckwith to Europe, he, with many of his company, volunteered to form part of the Rifle Brigade, an army then but lately added to the service; with this very company he was the first to be engaged with the enemy on board the *Elephant*, at Copenhagen, under the eye of Nelson himself, who, from that day forward, retained for him a warm and steady friendship.

"This brilliant success was followed by rapid promotion; he shared with the Rifle Brigade in their various and distinguished services, and met, in their command, the approbation and praise of the first captain of the day.

"That the loss of Sir Sidney Beckwith has been felt by all ranks, the mention of his name in any circle is sufficient to prove, and that this regret has extended to the highest ranks in the Presidency, we beg leave to quote the words of a letter we have seen from our present Governor:—

"'It is my most earnest wish and desire, both as regards Lady Beckwith and the members of Sir Sidney's family, to do everything in my power that may show the high respect I entertain for his truly noble character, and how deeply I lament his loss.'"

"In concluding this short memoranda of the public life of our late Governor, we cannot, but express our gratification in learning that it is the intention of many of the leading members of society to commemorate, in a suitable manner, the melancholy event, and that a monument is to be erected where he was buried on the summit of the Mahabaleshwar hills."

Not only that Sir Sidney Beckwith was held in profound respect for his virtues and character at the time of his death, but even now his Monument is held in great reverence by the lower classes of people at Mahabaleshwar, who actually worship it as a god and offer their prayers to it.

2. Bombay Point.

Bombay Point is one of the most popular and oldest points at Mahabaleshwar. It owes its existence to Dr. James Murray, who was the Superintendent of Mahabaleshwar in early thirties. It being on the old road to Bombay was called the "Bombay Point," and is known at Mahabaleshwar by that name since 1836. The view from this point is by far the most extensive and beautiful, and has rendered the place a most frequented rendezvous. From this point the sunset over the sea is most enjoyable as it glitters radiantly towards the declining and setting sun. It is therefore called the "Sunset Point." A large space was specially cleared up here for carriages, and a regular platform was also raised for a Band. Formerly it was considered a most popular place of amusement in the evening. It has, however, now lost its former importance owing to the formation of clubs and gymkhanas elsewhere on these hills; yet it attracts a large number of visitors to view the glorious sunset, which is a most charming sight at Mahabaleshwar. Sir George Birdwood, an enthusiastic admirer of Mahabaleshwar, has given a very graphic description of this point, which I cull from his interesting book "SVA":—

"Bombay Point is so called from its having been there that the plateau of Mahabaleshwar was first reached by the old road from Bombay up the Rotunda Ghaut. It is a large space cleared out of a wood of noble evergreen trees, and fenced in, above the Rotunda Pass, by a low parapet, overgrown with Clematis wightiana (*Murvail*), Hoya viridiflora (*Hirandori*), the sweet-scented, white-flowered Jasminum latifolium (*Kusur*), Embelia Basaal (*Ambut*), and other luxuriant creepers and scandent shrubs. The view from it is the most extensive and varied and the most interesting on the hill; and hence this green, cool, and fragrant spot is the general resort, of an afternoon, towards sundown, of the English families residing during the hot season at Mahabaleshwar. It is evergreen-wooded down to its base, in the sweet valley of the Koyna, west of which the rugged, craggy spurs of the Sahyadris, stretching across the Konkan, present an infinite diversity of picturesque contours, spur beyond spur, without end, toward the north and south, and only bounded on the west by the glittering horizon of the Arabian Sea. It is said that sometimes a glimpse may be obtained, beyond the long sylvan valley of the Nagotna river, of Bombay, 100 miles distant as the crow flies; while southward the coast can be followed to Ratnagiri.

"In the middle ground the low saddle-backed ridge, dipping down from Elphinstone Point, and forming the western enclosure of the Koyna valley at its head, suddenly ascends, before dipping down again to the Par Ghat, in Sivaji's massive flat-topped hill fort of Pratabgar. Only 4 miles distant, and rising by steep grassy slopes to an altitude of 3,543 feet above the Arabian Sea, distinctly visible on the left, it stands out boldly against the blue sky, directly in front of Bombay Point, and in strong contrast, when, after mid-day, its whole eastward side is in shade, with the bright, shining heights of the Konkans beyond. As the rays of after-noon sun begin gradually to strike more and more horizontally through the heated, rarefied mists drawn up by it during the forenoon, the natural complexion of this majestic scene undergoes a series of atmospheric transfigurations of indescribable splendour. At first the hills and dales of the Konkans seem to be suddenly transmuted into silver, shining, as with its own light, in dazzling brightness along the ridges of the hills, but with a softer lustre in the dales; where their ethereal illumination is subdued by the lengthening shadows thrown by the sinking sky. Again, in the twinkling of an eye, all is changed to radiant gold, clear as topaz on the hill-tops, with the sea on the left ruled in long levelled lines of chrysolite. When the day closes upon the eastern hemisphere, the rapidly falling mists pass from a glowing purple to dense indigo, and the cleared sky at last reflects back from the darkened landscape the deep transparent sapphire colour that is the proper tincture of an Indian night."

3. The Connaught Peak.

No other point on the hills presents sunrise and sunset in their varied beauty to the beholder's eye so effectively as the Connaught Peak. Being 4,644 feet above sea-level, the highest point on the hills, and situated between two deep valleys, the Krishna on one side, and the Koyna on the other, the Connaught Peak naturally commands the most magnificent and inspiring scenery that was ever presented to the human eye. This small, open plateau, which was known for many years as "Mount Olympia," was named "Connaught Peak" by Dr. Dimmoch, Superintendent of Mahabaleshwar, after His Royal Highness the Duke of Connaught, who was Commander-in-Chief of the Bombay Army from 1886-1890. It is indeed very difficult, nay, almost impossible, to bring out in words an exact picture of the extensive and wonderful panorama that is unrolled before our eyes, as we stand on the Peak.

The task, however, has been very ably achieved by Captain Medows Taylor in the following words:—

"It is almost impossible to convey by description any adequate idea of its peculiar character, or of the beauty of the ever-changing aerial effects, that vary in aspect almost as the spectator turns from one point to another. Often in early morning, as the sun rises over the lower mists, the naked peaks and precipices, standing apart like islands, glisten with rosy tints, while the mist itself, as yet dense and undisturbed, lies wrapped around their bases, filling every ravin and valley and glittering like a sea of molten silver.

"Again as the morning breeze rises in the valleys below, this vapour breaks up slowly: circling round the mountain summits, lingering in wreaths among their glens and precipices, and clinging to the forests, until dissipated entirely by the fierce beams, of the sun. Then quivering under the fervid heat, long ridges of rugged valleys are spread out below, and range beyond range melts tenderly into a dim distance of sea and sky, scarcely separated in colour, yet showing the occasional sparkle of a sail, like a faint cloud passing on the horizon. Most glorious of all, perhaps, in the evening, when, in the rich colours of the fast-rising vapours, the mountains glow like fire; and peak and precipice, forest and glen, are bathed in gold and crimson light; or as the light glows dimmer, shrouded in deep purple shadow till they disappear in the gloom which quickly falls on all."

There is a fine road upto the foot of the Connaught Peak and thence a very easy ascent to the summit. On the top of the plateau there is a dias covered with a bower of creepers in the centre which renders the place very enjoyable, especially in the cool hours of the morning and evening.

4. Elphinstone Point and Arthur's Seat.

"Elphinstone Point" is the first point opened up on these hills by Dr. James Murray in 1830, and named after the Hon. Sir Mountstuart Elphinstone, famous Governor of the Bombay Presidency. The distance between Elphinstone Point and Frere Hall is only seven miles, and Arthur's Seat is two miles further off from the former. The cliffs at these points are higher than at any of the nearer eminences. They rise from the Konkan which is some two thousand five hundred feet below the level of the Koyna valley. The ravine between Elphinstone Point and Arthur's Seat is the rise of the river Savitri, and the height of the cliff at the point where the stream reaches its base, is not less than 3,000 feet. "Nothing can be finer," writes Dr. James Murray in 1830, "than the scenery of this place, having for its climax the magnificent view from the extreme end of the headland. From this point, as from the top of Radtonda Ghaut, we overlook the Konkan spread out beneath our feet, with all its apparently diminutive mountains and glistening rivers, bordered by a large expanse of sea on the horizon, on which, in clear weather, ships may be very plainly discerned with the naked eye. So precipitous is the cliff, that, standing on the verge, its base is not seen; but the eye, in looking over, falls at once on the valley of the Savitree, at the terrific depth of full three thousand feet. An abrupt range of bare black peaks, of a singularly wild and savage character, forms the further side of this stupendous chasm."

From Elphinstone Point to Arthur's Seat the road runs close to the edge of the cliffs from which a small stone parapet only divides it. Arthur's Seat is the highest point of the range in the neighbourhood, being 4,421 feet above sea-level. The view from this point is very extensive and commanding. It is generally believed that the place was called 'Arthur's Seat' after the name of Mr. Arthur Malet (son of Sir Charles Malet, first Resident at the Peshwa's court at Poona) who first built a house at Mahabaleshwar. But it is said to be incorrect. The spot was called 'Arthur's Seat' after the illustrious name of Sir George Arthur who was Governor of Bombay from 1841 to 1846. Mr. Arthur Malet, who was for many years Secretary to Government and also Member of Council, was no doubt a famous person who figured on the Mahabaleshwar hills in the fifties. His name was celebrated on these hills by calling another spot "Malet Point," which is only a few yards distant from Arthur's Seat.

"From Arthur's Seat north-westward," writes Sir George Birdwood, "across the dense forest that shelters the sources of the Krishna, extends the main axis of the Sahyadris; their blackened, trackless gorges, and bluffs of stratified basalt, stratum upon stratum, high uplifted to the zenith, and gigantic stacks of serried peaks, presenting, as thus viewed foreshortened, a boundless prospect of the wildest desolation."

The forest near this point is called *Brahmaranya* or "the forest of the God Brahma." It immensly adds to the wildness of the scenery. About half a mile from Arthur's Seat, a small path leads down to a spring, 200 feet below, generally called "Tiger's Spring." The path follows the line of the cliffs and joins another path which goes down to a small ledge known as the "window." It gives a magnificent view of the extraordinary drop into the valley below.

There were formerly two bungalows for the visitors, one at the Arthur's Seat and one at the Malet Point. Both of them are not now in existence. There is a fine bungalow newly built for visitors by the Municipality at the Elphinstone Point, which is generally used for picnic parties. A fee of Rs. 3 per day is charged for its use.

5. Kate's Point.

This point, locally known as Nak Khind, is named after Kate, a daughter of Sir John Malcolm. It is well-known more for its huge and very remarkably shaped rock which stands majestically on the hills on the right side of the Krishna valley, than for the view seen therefrom, though

KATE'S POINT, MAHABALESHWAR.

the latter is no less extensive and grand than that seen from other points. This tremendous rock is at the extremity of the point which rises perpendicular on one side over the valley of the Krishna, and falls gradually on the other into platforms of the rocks, which render it perfectly accessible to man. This rock is about hundred feet high, and appears to have become detached from the main portion. A few smaller boulders, wedged between this rock and the face of the cliff form a connecting link, not more than six feet wide, requiring steadiness to cross. The rock and scarp with the connecting boulders form a curious natural arch, admitting a distinct view of the mountain-ridges behind it. The two rocks thus joined, suggest the likeness of the head of an elephant with his trunk hanging down. The want of variety and grandeur possessed by other hills is made up here by the splendid valley of the Krishna below, which, with its zigzag and slender course and patches of cultivation on both sides, presents a scenery peculiar to itself. From here we get a view of the Deccan side, which is available from no other point on the hills. The prominent objects in the landscape here are three fine heights, Kamalgad, Pandavgad and Mandhardeva.

6. The Krishna Temple.

The village of Mahabaleshwar lies about three miles to the north of the present Sanitarium, Malcolm Peith. It is considered a *kshetra* or sacred place by the Hindus, as it is situated at the source of the holy river Krishna. There is another temple dedicated to the God Mahadev at this village, known as 'Mahableshwar,' which gives its name to the village and generally to these hills. The principal place of worship, however, is the temple of the river Krishna, which is also called "the Panchaganga temple," as the other four holy rivers, besides the Krishna, namely, Koyana, Yenna, Gayatri and Savitri, are said to take their source from here. This temple is held in great reverence by the Hindus, who visit it on pilgrimage and bathe in the holy waters of the river Krishna. The greatest number of pilgrims resort to this place on *kanyagat*, every twelfth year, when the planet Jupitar enters the sign of Virgo. It is credulously believed that on this occasion the great river Ganga (Ganges) comes here to meet her younger sister Krishna, and remains here for a period of twelve months.

The temple dedicated in honour of the river Krishna is said to be built first by

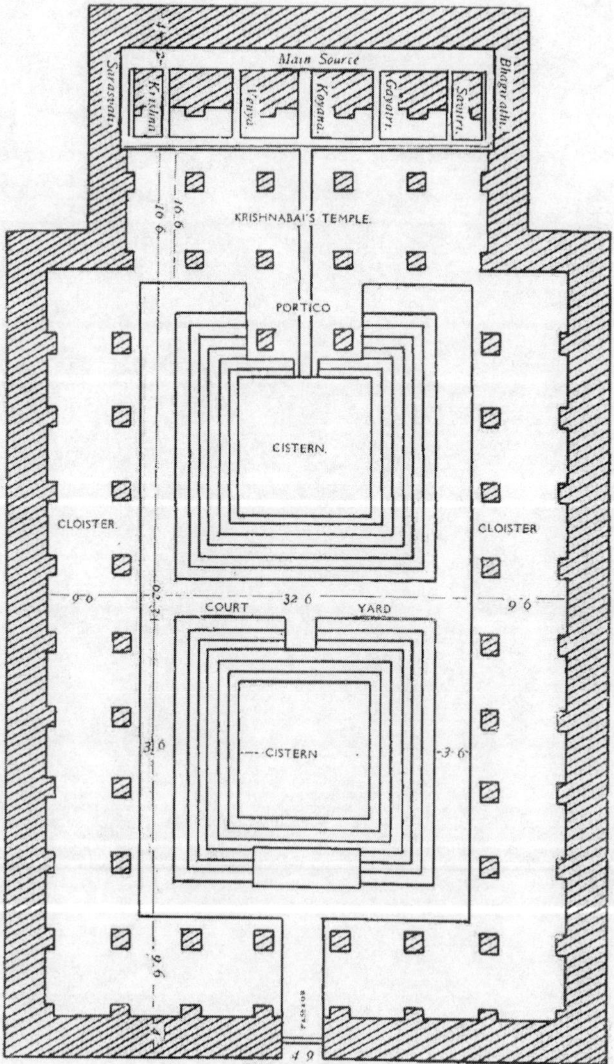

SKETCH OF THE KRISHNA TEMPLE.

Chandra Rao More, Raja of Jaoli, who was an influencial Maratha nobleman in the service of the king of Bijapur, who ruled over the country in the early part of the 17th century. It was subsequently improved and enlarged by Raja Shivaji and his mother Jijabai, who held this place in great sanctity and occasionally visited it. In the middle of the 18th century, the temple gave way owing to the heavy rainfall, and was rebuilt by Parashram Ramchandra Angal, a rich banker of Satara. Lastly, in 1875, the Chief of Jamkhindi at the expense of Rs. 15,000 made certain repairs and covered the courtyard with corrugated iron sheets for the convenience of bathing people; but it has prevented the sun from sending its purifying rays inside, though sky light is taken from above. The temple is built of black trap and is a large one. The following description of it is given by the late Rao Saheb V. N. Mandlik of Bombay in 1870:—

"The temple stands at the foot of the hill facing the east, and with its auxiliary buildings occupies an area of about 6,000 square feet enclosed by masonry walls 4 feet in thickness. The temple measures 36′ 6″ in length and 16′ 6″ in breadth, having an open courtyard in front, measuring 62′ 3″ in length and 32′ 6″ in width, which contains two cisterns having flights of steps leading down to their bottoms. Along the three sides of the courtyard is a cloister 9′ 6″ in width, with pillars 2′ square in front. In the Eastern face of the cloister is an entrance gate 4′ 9″ in width, with a passage of the same width leading to the courtyard. By the sides of the cloisters, the visitors pass over a broad step and approach the temple. The plinth of the temple, as well as of the cloisters, is raised 3 feet above that of the courtyard and their floors paved with cut stone. The temple is formed of two bays, with a portico in front. Each bay is divided into five parts, each 7′ 6″ in length, from centre to centre of the pillars, which measure 4½ feet from the surface of the floor. Semi-circular arches have been turned both longitudinally and transversely as shown by dotted lines on the plan. The construction of the roof is peculiar. Each subdivision of the bay forms a square, and is separately roofed in by brackets or corbels placed over the crown of the arches, the upper bracket projecting beyond the one just below it, thus forming a dome. The roof, therefore, when seen from inside, shows as many domes as there are subdivisions in each bay; while the outside of the roof has been brought in a line and finished off in steps running longitudinally, but sloping transversely to carry down rain-water. The construction of the roof of the cloisters is similar to that of the temple. To the west side of the temple, and between the two walls, is the main source. Through the front wall, five holes or drains have been made, which represent the rivers Krishna, Venna, Koyana, Gayatri and Savitri. The priests say, that two other rivers, namely, the Bhagirathi and the Saraswati, flow from the two sides of the other Gangas or rivers,—the former, once in every twelve years, as has been above described; and the latter, once in every sixty years. These holes, through which these two rivers are said to flow, are marked on the plan in the north and south corners respectively.

"The water from the main source flows through the above mentioned five holes into a channel in their front, and ultimately discharges itself through a spout, resembling a cow's head, into the cistern in the courtyard. Here the visitors to the temple bathe and perform all the ceremonies connected with their ablutions. The walls and roof of the temple, &c., are of a permanent construction. Cut stone has been used throughout, and the building has a bold cornice all round."*

The water from the mouth of the cow, which is called *gomukha*, falls into the cistern below, which then goes into the other cistern. The first or upper cistern is used for bathing by the Hindus of the higher classes, and the second by those of the lower ones. On account of the sanctity of this place the Mahabaleshwar village is regarded by Hindus as a क्षेत्र or holy place; and all the Hindus of Malcom Peith and neighbouring villages come here to perform religious rites, which forms a source of income to the Brahmin priests and other servants of the temple residing there. The first hereditary officer connected with the management of the temple is a Koli by caste, who receives the offerings made by pilgrims to the river Krishna. There are two yearly festivals (उत्सव) held in honour of the river Krishna, once in फाल्गुन (February or March), and again in आश्विन, (September or October), which is known as नवरात्रोत्सव. To defray the expenses of these festivals the Raja of Satara has endowed the village of Kharshi

---

* The Writings and Speeches of the late Rao Saheb V. N. Mandlik, C.S.I., pages 269, 290.

KRISHNA TEMPLE, MAHABALESHWAR.

(INNER VIEW.)

to the temple of the river Krishna, yielding an annual revenue of about Rs. 500.

The temple being a तीर्थ or a sacred place, only the Hindus are allowed to enter it. Non-Hindus can only view it from the entrance. In order to give an adequate idea of the temple, the inside springs of the Krishna and other four rivers, and the two cisterns or holy pools, a sketch has been affixed hereto, which will help the visitor,—especially the non-Hindu visitor, who cannot enter the precincts of the temple.

The river Krishna apparently ceases to flow from the main temple; but it again appears at another temple, which is built by Shivaji on a steep rock at a little distance from the chief temple. The Krishna falls into the valley below, which takes her name and is called the "Krishna Valley." The view from this place of the deep valley is simply magnificent. "Few scenes," writes Mrs. Postans in 1838, "are more lovely than the beautiful valley of the Krishna, as seen from the open temples of Mahabaleshwar. The smooth and brightly gleaming waters, like a silvery thread, wind their quiet way between the richly-wooded hills, which form a vista of fertile shelter to the grassy banks; while the herds, feeding peacefully beside the sacred river, complete the scene and afford a glimpse of pastoral beauty, the more fair and sweet, perhaps, as contrasted with the sublime mountain solitudes of the immediate neighbourhood."

7. The Temple of Mahabaleshwar.

The temple of Mahabaleshwar is a few yards distant from the temple of the river Krishna. It was first built by Raja Singhan, the famous king of the Yadav dynasty of Devgiri, who flourished in the 13th century. It was repaired by Raja Chandra Rao More of Jaoli at the end of the 16th century; and on the downfall of the Mores in 1655, it was improved and enlarged by Raja Shivaji, the founder of the Maratha Empire. It was again repaired by Raja Shahu (1708-1749); and lastly, it was rebuilt by Parshram Narayan Angal, a wealthy banker of Satara at the end of the 18th century. This banker is said to have spent considerable money in charity. The old temple was built after the style of Hemadpant, which can be clearly seen from the old foundations that are still visible around the main building. Owing to the excessive rainfall at Mahabaleshwar, it was quite natural that the building should have suffered so many times from climatic effects. The present temple

Village Temples, Mahabaleshwar.

was also repaired and a new *sabhamandap* was added to it some fifty years ago; but the latter is so ugly that it has marred the beauty of the main building.

The present temple of Mahabaleshwar is surrounded by a stone wall about five feet high. The main temple is built of black trap and is divided into two apartments, the inner room or God Chamber, and the outer room or Central Hall. Though the building was re-built by Raja Shahu's banker, Parsharam Narayan Angal, its structure retains inside the Hemadpanti style of Southern India temples. The temple is dedicated to God Shiva and a *ling* worship is performed here. The traditional account of the temple is given in the *Mahabaleshwar Puran*. It is as follows:—

"Two *Rakshasas* or demon brothers, named Mahabal and Atibal, bitter enemies of the Brahmins and their Gods, were so powerful and warlike that they disturbed the devotions of the Brahmins and harassed the people. The Brahmins appealed to Vishnu, who came and killed the younger brother Atibal. Enraged at the death of his brother, Mahabal challenged the God to single combat. They fought so long that Vishnu became exhausted and sought the help of the Goddess of Enchantment. She cast a spell over the giant so that he ceased fighting and promised to grant any favour the God should ask of him. The favour asked by the God was the death of Mahabal. As Mahabal had pledged his word, this favour had to be granted; and the God began to cut the giant in pieces without his offering any resistance. Struck with admiration, Shiva offered to fulfil any of his dying wishes. Several requests were made and granted, the chief being that Shiva and Vishnu should take the names of the giant and his brother, and that in memory of their fight their shrines should be called Mahabaleshwar and Atibaleshwar."*

The first worshippers of God Mahabaleshwar were Kolis, a hill tribe, who yet hold a hereditary position in the temple of Mahabaleshwar, as well as in that of the Krishna river. The name of the first Koli, as is given in old papers, was Babaji Koli, who was appointed manager of the temple by Raja Singhan (A.D. 1210–1247). His descentants enjoyed the right continuously under the rule of the Shirkes and the Mores. One of the descendants of Babaji Koli introduced a Gurav to worship the

* *Satara Gazetteer*, page 511.

God, probably in the middle of the 17th century. The right of worship in the temple of Mahabaleshwar has since been enjoyed by the Guravs. During the struggle between Chandra Rao More and Raja Shivaji, the valuable treasures of Jaoli were kept in the custody of Kanhoji Koli, who was granted by Chandra Rao an annual allowance of Rs. 60 and some grain and lands in addition. This person assisted Chandra Rao by supplying Guravs to carry on his secret correspondence to Bijapur. After the downfall of Chandra Rao More, Shivaji appears to have punished the Kolis and appointed Guravs as the chief worshippers of the God Mahableshwar, who were again confirmed in their duties by Ramchandra Pant Amatya (1672–1720). On the return of Raja Shahu to Satara in 1708, Suryaji Koli, one of the descendants of Babaji Koli, appealed to Satara king to make inquiry of his watan, and obtained a decision in his favour. He was again appointed the manager of the temple and the valuables belonging to the shrine were ordered to be kept in his custody. But the Guravs being dissatisfied with the decision killed Suryaji Koli. Vithal Gopal, Subhedar of Jaoli and Par, arrested the Guravs and sent them to Satara for trial.

Raja Shahu of Satara taking pity on these persons in the light of their being religious worshippers of God Mahabaleshwar, gave them a light punishment of *khoda*. They were kept in confinement at Par for sometime and were afterwards released. From this time the importance of Kolis ceased at Mahabaleshwar and the Guravs enjoy the right of worshipping the God without any interruption.

The temple has an endowment granted by Raja Shivaji and his descendants, which is continued to this day by the British Government. The villages assigned to the temple of Mahabaleshwar yield an annual revenue of Rs. 1,200, and the forest and other lands fetch about Rs. 2,000, which make up a total income of Rs. 3,200. This amount is utilised in defraying the expenses of the temple and the annual festivals.

The temple possesses a few old articles, which are still valued as historical relics. The silver image of Bhavani-Shankar, which was formerly dedicated to God Mahabaleshwar by Raja Chandra Rao More, was in the custody of the temple for two centuries, but was afterwards stolen and lost. It was replaced by a new one by the descendants of Chandra Rao More, who have now removed it to their village, Dare, where they keep it in their safe custody. They bring it every year to Mahabaleshwar with great ceremony at the time of the festival of *Shivratra*, for which they receive certain honours from the temple. The Mores who are now called 'Darekars' are still considered to be the chief devotees of God Mahabaleshwar and special regard is shown to them at the time of the festivals. This custom has been observed to this day to preserve their ancestral dignity and their close connection with the temple.

There are certain brass utensils presented by the Mores to God Mahabaleshwar, which are worth-seeing as historical mementos of that ancient family. Amongst these there is a brass cobra which is remarkable for its workmanship and its heavy weight. The following Sanskrit lines are inscribed on it:—

॥ श्री शके १५६६ तारण संवत्सरे श्रावण वदि
पंचमी सोमे नागार्पणं कृतं शिव पाहि ॥

This inscription gives the correct date Shake 1566 (A. D. 1644) of its presentation. The glittering spires of the temple, which are guilded in gold, were presented by Shivaji to God Mahabaleshwar after the death of Afzul Khan in 1659. They possess great historical value and are unique trophies of that famous event.

Near the temple of Mahabaleshwar there is another temple, called Atibaleshwar, which was also rebuilt by Parashram Narayan Angal of Satara. There is another temple, called Kedareshwar, built by the celebrated Queen Ahalyabai Holkar of Indore.

It may be also noted here that a small temple was erected in honour of the river Yenna (within one-fourth of a mile from the Yenna Lake) and an image was placed in it by Shrimant Chintaman Rao Appa Saheb Patwardhan, the grandfather of the present enlightened Chief of Sangli, who bears the same name. This is the third temple dedicated to a river at Mahabaleshwar.

8. The Manikbai and Gangabai Hindu Sanatorium.

This Sanatorium is situated at the old Mahabaleshwar on a very beautiful and picturesque site and is called "The Manikbai and Gangabai Hindu Sanatorium." It was established by Shet Purshottam Vishram Mawji, J. P., a Bhattia philanthrophist of Bombay, with the object of alleviating human suffering by providing facilities to people of slender means to obtain the benefit of the invigorating

HINDU SANATORIUM, MAHABALESHWAR.

and salubrious climate of this celebrated health-resort during the period of illness and convalescence. The site selected for this useful institution is in every way convenient and suitable to the Hindu invalids who go there for the benefit of their health. There is abundant spring water, sufficient open space for long walks, and beautiful scenery. Besides these, there are the sacred shrines of the river Krishna and the God Mahabaleshwar in near vicinity, which to the Hindus are objects of spiritual and religious interest. The Sanatorium is divided into small blocks which are assigned to different families. For the comforts and recreation of the sick and the convalesent every care is taken. There is a charitable dispensary in charge of a qualified medical man and also a free library containing a good stock of selected books in English, Gujrathi and Marathi. This institution was opened by H. E. Sir George Sydenham Clarke (now Lord Sydenham), the then Governor of Bombay, on the 25th May 1910. Since then the institution has become very popular and is considered a boon to the Hindu invalids who resort to it.

9. Pratapgad.

Pratapgad, one of the famous forts of Shivaji, is eight miles west of Mahabaleshwar. It is 3,543 feet above sea-level. It is built on a range which forms the spur of the Mahableshwar hills and separates the villages of Par and Kineshwar. The situation of the fort is strategically important as it fully commands the high way to the Konkan. There is not a single pass between Pratapgad and the neighbouring hills, which is unprotected and easily accessible. Shivaji pitched upon the high commanding and flat-topped rock to secure access to his territories on the Nira and the Koyana, and to strengthen the defences of the Par Pass, which was the only practicable route for carrying cattle and guns in ancient times. The original name of this hill was *Dhorapya Dongar.* It was in the possession of the Shirkes and the Mores, the Maratha rulers of the Konkan. After the conquest of the kingdom of Chandra Rao More, Shivaji undertook the work of fortifying this hill fort and entrusted it to his faithful Brahmin officer, Moro Trimal Pingle, who afterwards rose to great distinction and became the Prime Minister of Shivaji. More Trimal Pingle completed this work satisfactorily in 1656. He built a

PRATAPGAD FORT WITH AFZUL KHAN'S TOMB.

double line of fortifications on the top of the hill and guarded it by bastions on each corner. It was done so skilfully that the fort was considered quite impregnable in those days. The strong massive walls built on the steep precipices, the huge gates studded with gigantic iron spikes, the projecting towers and commanding bastions rendered it one of the strongest hill forts of the Deccan, which strengthened the power of Shivaji in the Konkan.

Pratapgad is most conspicuous in the history of the Marathas on account of the well-known and tragic espisode of the death of Afzul Khan in 1659. The place selected by Shivaji for the interview with Afzul Khan is below the fort on the crest of a lofty eminence and possesses a most romantic and wild scenery. In the Koyana valley down below, the army of the Khan was encamped on the banks of the river. The Khan ascended the hill in a palanquin by a special route made by Shivaji through the thickly wooded jungle. A shamiana platform was raised on the spot, which was covered with a beautiful and costly silken tent. This spot can be now seen at the foot of the hill, which is surrounded by green forest of awe-inspiring silence, occasionally broken by sweet notes of birds in the glens. The spot is yet honoured by annually taking to it the palanquin of the Goddess Bhavani on the Dassera day and worshipping it there. At this time some offerings are made to the tomb of Afzul Khan as a mark of respect to the fallen hero.

The fort of Pratapgad consists of two parts—the lower fort and the upper fort. The latter is generally known as "Balekilla" or inner fort. It is built upon the crest of the hill, 200 yards long and 200 yards wide. It contained some permanent residential buildings. Shivaji built his own palace here as well as a temple of Shiva called "Kedareshwar," which was the presiding deity of this mountain. Shivaji respected it highly and gave a grant for its management.

The chief temple at Pratapgad is that of Bhavani, the family goddess of Shivaji. It is on the eastern side of the fort. It was built by Shivaji in 1661. There is a traditional story that Shivaji first dedicated a temple to goddess Ramvardayani Devi of Chandra Rao More on the fort, and intended to build a new temple for his family Goddess Bhavani of Tuljapur at Raygad and establish its image there.

Afzul Khan's Tomb at Pratapgad.

The Goddess, it is said, appeared in Shivaji's dream and told him that she would be pleased if her image was worshipped at Pratapgad. Shivaji obeyed the divine orders and dedicated to her a new temple at Pratapgad. Shivaji and his mother often visited the temple and stayed at Pratapgad. It was the custom of his family to pay their respects to the Goddess and perform her *puja* once a year. The name of the priest who was appointed by Shivaji to worship the Goddess was Vishwanath Bhat Hadap, whose descendants still perform that duty.

The original temple of Bhavani is built of black trap and is 171 feet in length and 104½ feet in breadth. It is divided into two chambers, the God Chamber and the Central Hall. The wooden *sabha-mandap* is a modern addition made by Raja Pratap Sing of Satara (1818–39). He covered the main temple with copper sheets at a great cost in order to protect it from heavy rains. The temple is worth a visit on account of its historical associations. It possesses some old ornaments, lace clothes and silver utensils, which are worth inspection. There is a precious crystal *ban* which Shivaji used to worship himself. For the expenses of the temple and its annual festivals 15 villages have been granted as *inam* by Shivaji and his descendants, which yield an annual revenue of Rs. 2,000. There are two lamp-pillars called *dipmalas* in front of the temple, which were struck by lightning and partly broken some years ago. Their workmanship is considered to be of a superior order.

The upper fort contained several buildings such as granneries, magazines, stables, but now they are all in ruins. The old ramparts and bastions as well as old gates and tanks give some idea of its former greatness and remind the visitor of its past glory. There are only a few houses in the fort, which contain a population of about 75 souls, mostly belonging to the temple.

The fort of Pratapgad is within an easy reach of Mahabaleshwar. There is an excellent road from Malcolm Peith to Vada or Ambenali about 10 miles, which is an hour's drive by the picturesque Fitzgerald Ghaut. At Vada there is a comfortable bungalow for travellers in a shady place, from which the historic fort of Pratapgad can be easily ascended on foot. Chairs with bearers are also available in the season and the rates of hire are fixed. The ascent is not very difficult though the road is not smooth and fine. It is however shady and thickly wooded, and the troubles are repaid by the historical sights and romantic scenery.

10. Sidney or Lodwick Point.

Sidney or Lodwick Point was formerly known only by the name of Sidney Point, but latterly it received the name of Lodwick Point, when a monument in honour of General Lodwick was raised here by his son, Mr. R. W. Lodwick, Bombay Civil Service, in 1874, with the permission of the Bombay Government. The memory of Sir Sidney Beckwith has been cherished on the Mahabaleshwar hills in another place, which is well-known as "Beckwith Monument." The name Sidney was given to this point by Dr. James Murray as early as 1832, but was changed to Lodwick Point in 1874. This change was not liked by many. Dr. Wilson, the famous missionary of Bombay, was one of those who used humorously to resent such "tampering with historical and landscape associations." But the name, "Lodwick Point," has now become well-known and popular on these hills on account of the general impression created by the inscription that Lodwick was the first English gentleman who climbed the hill. This impression is obviously wrong as will be seen from the second chapter of this book. But, '*Aldinis falsis animus meliora recasut*'—the mind attracted by what is false has no relish for better things. The knowledge of true history will, however, vanquish all false ideas in the end.

The Lodwick Point is about three miles north-east of Malcolm Peith. The extreme end of the Point, known as the "Nose," is 4,067 feet above sea-level. The carriage road runs up to the foot of the rising promontory on which Lodwick Monument has been placed. From this Monument to the extreme end is a sort of narrow wall of basalt, not more than 6 to 12 feet broad towards its extremity, which forms a natural bridge with a deep drop on each side. The "Nose" or the end of the point is only 12 feet wide, which drops down suddenly into the valley of the river Koyana, below 2,500 feet. The drop is so perpendicular that a run-away horse was seen by Sir George Birdwood (while in India, 1854–1868) leaping at full gallop from the point and falling dead at its base without striking against any salient ledge or angle in the fall. This point is considered most beautiful by some, though the view

LODWICK MONUMENT, MAHABALESHWAR.

is less extensive on either side than from several other points. "Projecting out into the sky," writes Sir George Birdwood, "almost like a bowsprit from a ship, it commands a lofty perspective of the Konkans, in front of the main axis of the Sahyadris; but the predominant feature in the landscape here is the point itself, rearing it's colossal wall, like a horse's neck thrown up inquiringly, above the deep, beautiful-wooded ravines of the Koyna on either side of it." The picturesque and historic Pratapgad in the front, on the left and immediately in the valley below, the serpentine and zigzag windings of the Fitzgerald Ghaut, above it the beautiful Bombay Point, and some miles straight off the lofty Saddle-Back hill; and on the right, the Elphinstone Point and its crags, and down below, the deep ravines, crowded with rugged cliffs, dense forests, and glittering streams, all these present a most attractive scene.

The Lodwick Monument is a column erected in 1874 on the top of the hill, which is about 25 feet high from the ground to the top of the urn which surmounts the pillar. On the west of the base of this Monument is the head of General Lodwick sculptured in alto-relievo in white marble, protected by strong tin wire in an iron frame. On the three sides of the column the following inscriptions are given:—

On the south side is written:

"In memory of
General Peter Lodwick
Second son of John Lodwick, Esq., S. Shoebury, Essex,
who entered the Hon. E. I. Co's. Service in 1799,
and died at Bagneres de Bigorre, France,
August 28th, 1873,
aged 90.

Senior Officer of H. M.'s Forces in India."

On the east side is written:

"In 1803-04, he saw service as a Subaltern in connection with the operations of the Army under Sir Arthur Wellesley. He was Brigade Major of Captain Ford's Subsidiary Force at the Battle of Kirkee, November 5th, 1817, when 2,800 British troops defeated the Peishwa's Army, and was present at the taking of Purandhar and other hill forts. He commanded a Regiment at Kittur in 1824; he subsequently became Town Major of Bombay; and closed his career in India as Resident of Satara."

"The first European who set foot on these hills, he made known salubrity of the climate, and led to the establishment of the Mahabaleshwar Sanitarium, thus conferring an inestimable benefit on the Bombay Presidency."

On the north side is written:

"This point, now by order of Government designated Lodwick Point in honour of his name, he reached alone in 1827, after hours of toil through the dense forest. Here, therefore, as the most appropriate spot this monument has, with the permission of Government, been erected by his own son, R. W. Lodwick, of Her Majesty's Bombay Civil Service, Accountant General of Madras, in 1874."

The date 1827 given in the above inscription is incorrect, as Lodwick first visited this place in 1824, when he was a Commanding Officer at Satara.

II. Water-falls.

There are three chief water-falls on the Mahabaleshwar hills. They are well worth a visit, especially in the cold weather when the volume of water is considerable. (1) The Yenna falls, (2) the Chinaman's falls, and (3) Dhobi's falls. The Yenna falls are in the Yenna valley near Lingmala, and are by far the best. The Chinaman's falls are in the ravine between the Sassoon and Falkland Points near the gardens formerly cultivated by the Chinese ticket-of-leave men, to the south of the Malcolm Peith. The Dhobi's or washermen's water-falls are on the bridle-path connecting the Sideny Point with the Elphinstone Point and the old Mahabaleshwar Road. These falls though insignificant are situated in a lovely sequestered nook looking straight at the south side of the Elphinstone Point ravine. The rocks on either side are abrupt and lofty, while there is abundance of foliage that adds to the beauty of the scenery. The falls of the Yenna river are very beautiful and their sight in the cold weather is very attractive. Dr. Murray gives the following graphic description of these falls which is very interesting:—

"The river is here precipitated over the face of the cliffs, a sheer descent of five or six hundred feet, in a nearly uninterrupted fall when its stream is swollen by rain, but in its ordinary condition divided by projecting rocks about one-third down, and scattered below into thin white streaks and spray, which the oblique rays of the morning sun may often be seen circling with rain-bows. A visit to this spot in rainy weather, or on any clear day in the monsoon, will amply repay the admirer of the wilder beauties of nature. The headlong rush and roar of the falling river, the thousand other silvery streams everywhere seaming the steep dark sides of the chasm, as they hasten to join the foaming torrent, which, far below, is dashing impetuously on through masses of opposing rock, the grandeur of the whole surrounding scenery, now hid, now half revealed, now bright in sun-shine, as the floating mists alternately envelope the valley or are rolled away and dispersed by the breeze—all combine to form a scene of the most interesting and absorbing character, such as few can bring themselves to quit without an effort."

"From this point, the road winds along the top of the cliff, crosses the river, now flowing through overhanging woods and rocks, above the waterfall, ascends to a sweetly situated village on the opposite bank, where the dog-rose is found growing to all appearance wild, and enters a closely wooded old avenue, skirted by most picturesque forest dingle, and opening at length on smooth green meadows and luxuriant willows, through which the Yenna is again seen sluggishly winding."

The forest bungalow of Lingmala is close by. Lingmala is the site of the cinchona plantation that was specially undertaken by Government in 1865 and continued till 1875, but without success. When it proved unremunerative, it was transferred to the Forest Department. A sum of Rs. 64,000 was spent on this project, but its return was nominal. The cause of its failure was attributed to the decay of the plants owing to the dryness of weather followed by excessive rain.

Besides the places of interest described above, there are several other points and objects which may be found interesting by visitors; but it is not possible to refer to them in the limited space of this book beyond simply mentioning their names. Among them may be mentioned the Carnac, Falkland, Sassoon, Babington, Hunter, Helen's, and Northcote Points; the Robber's Caves, Government House, Mount Malcolm, Church, Cemetry; European, Hindu and Parsi Gymkhana Clubs, &c. Besides these there are many places in the neighbourhood, such as Makarandgad or Saddle-Back, Parut, Bamnoli, Chanda Kamalgad, and Kas Lake which offer great attraction to excursionists and sportsmen.

CHAPTER VI.

DISTINGUISHED VISITORS ON MAHABALESHWAR.

I

Perambulator.*

A.D. 1826.

We have often heard, my dear Mr. Editor, of the invigorating influence existing in the climate of the Nilgherry mountains, and its capabality of restoring energy to the debilitated constitutions of our tropical exiles; but, while the people of Bombay console themselves that they may there find relief from the misery of a hot season and a remedy in sickness, it will be pleasing to know that they might enjoy similar immunities injudiciously profitting from the advantages which a residence on the hills of Mahabillysir holds out to them during the months of March, April and May.

These hills are, I believe, little known; or if known, their climate is not as yet sufficiently appreciated, although a short account of it was inserted in your paper for 1824, by a gentleman who was among

---

* This is supposed to be the nom-de-plume of Dr. Bird, Residency Surgeon at Satara, who accompanied Col. Briggs to Mahabaleshwar in 1826 and contributed this article to the "Bombay Courier" on the 20th May 1826.

the first to derive no less benefit than pleasure from it during the hot season of that year.

The situation is almost equidistant from Mahar and Satara, and forming a table-land of nearly 5,000 feet, it gives rise to the different branches of the Krishna river, and is therefore the most elevated points of the Ghauts in these parts. The breadth of this table-land, from where the road beginning at the Ghaut leads from the valley of Satara until it again descends on the opposite side into Konkun, is about eight miles. The distance from Mahar to the hills is little more than thirty miles, or three stages.

I have seen the Madras reports of the Nilgherry hills of which the climate is colder than that of Mahabillysir and the elevation greater, I should think, by 3,000 feet; but, if permitted to institute a comparison and to speak theoretically, I should prefer that of the latter, as it is more temperate and therefore better suited to restore lost energy to invalids, debilitated from the effect of heat, and who require an immediate change.

Those who have enjoyed the usual cold weather of Deccan, during December and January, will be able to form a much better general idea of the Mahabillysir climate, from March to June, than could be possibly conveyed to them by any more minute or laboured description. The minimum of Fahrenheit's thermometer is sometimes, at night 64°; a range of temparature which is only four degrees less than the maximum heat, in May, on the Nilgherry hills.

Though the average heat at Mahabillysir, little after noon, is 80°, in a house or twelve degrees greater than the extreme heat of the Nilgherries, the temperature of the former, when there are clouds, does not exceed 70°; the average variation, during the day, is about 12° of Fahrenheit. The maximum in tents, for this month was sometimes above 80°; but this increase of heat seldom exceeded two hours' duration, and was not at any time oppressive nor exhausting, when the wind blows from the eastward the heat is greatest, and at such times the air is very dry. In general, however, it blows from the west, or north-west, white clouds which render the atmosphere damp and chilly. These fleecy masses of snow-like vapour, collecting over the deep ravines hang on the brows of the mountain summits, until the succeeding morning the Sun has acquired sufficient power to dissolve them; they are thus dissipated for a time, only again to reassemble when he shall have withdrawn his influence at his setting.

The soil of the hills is a red iron clay, which does not appear to communicate any chalybeate properties to the water of the place. The water, which is soft, and contains little or no gypsum, is found a few feet below the soil, where there are hollows and ravines.

The only inhabitants here are a few poor villagers, who smelt iron, and the Dunger tribes, or Cowherds, who live in small huts and pasture their cattle during the rains. These people report favourably of the healthiness of the climate even at that season when fevers are usually present in other hilly situations.

To those who are suffering more particularly from weakened stomach, general debility, and exhaustion, than from any specific visceral enlargement, a residence here during the hot season presents incalculable advantages when the secretion of the lever has been languid, it at first produces an irregular but augmented circulation in that organ, by increasing the tone and energy of the stomach; and to those who might have not access to a physician, it will be satisfactory to know, that a few grain doses of calomel, the daily application of warm bathing and the flesh-brush with the habitual use of flannel and warm clothing, are the proper correctives for this state until, by a longer residence here, the body shall have retrieved what it had previously lost in a too moist and heated atmosphere. Exercise, both on foot and horseback, can be freely indulged in; to which the invalid will be naturally prompted by the bracing influence of the air, and the encouragement of a good road for a morning ride, through romantic and picturesque scenery. To the sportsman these hills offer, I fear, but little amusement; a few hares, jungle and spur fowl, being the only game. But those to whom the voice of the Black-bird and Thrush can bring pleasing recollections, and who loved to associate the pleasures of a happier climate with the appearance of ferns, willows, and the moss in blossom, will find here no mean comparison, for India, of that climate, for which, as Englishmen, we all long after, not only in our sickness but in our exile. A small wooden bungalow, such as Colonel Briggs has lately built, or a temporary *chupper* over tent, would effectually secure people from any inconvenience during the day, when the thermometer exceeds 80° and as the nights are cold, blankets and warm clothing are indespensible requisites.

In conclusion, should this notice of Mahabillysir tempt any invalid to enjoy its climate, when circumstances do not admit him visiting that of England, it will be pleasing to think, that it has not been written in vain.—*Bombay Courier, 20-5-1826.*

2

Elizabeth Grant on Mahabaleshwar.

A.D. 1829.

*   *   *   *

Colonel Smith, who had been his (her fathers*) constant riding companion, had inspired him with a wish to see more of the country, to try a few weeks at the Mahableishwar Hills during the present hot season, when Bombay was really too oppressive. These charming hills were in our new friend's district; he commanded the brigade at Satara, and Mahableishwar, though thirty miles distant, was included. He had been eloquent in his description of the scenery, the lights and shadows, mists, and other phenomena, and had kindly offered every assistance as to preparations, routes, encampment there, etc.

My mother, who began to have her suspicions as to all this politeness, exhibited no wish to move; she

* Sir John Grant, who was Chief Justice of Bombay at this time (1829.)

did not feel it in the least too hot where she was, nor did she like the idea of packing, moving, going in boats, in palanquins, over the sea and up precipices, to live in tents without any comforts.

My father, however, was quite taken up with the plan; Colonel Smith dined two or three days running to concert all the arrangements, and then one morning he called to take leave. He was to start early next day for Mahableishwar, where he meant to remain till the rains began, would lose no time in doing—I forget what—choosing the spot for our tents, I believe, and would write full particulars of all we were to expect on our journey.

Preparations were accordingly begun; my father and his head servant Nasserwanjee were closeted for hours for several days, and at last all was announced as ready. The ayahs packed our clothes, taking a great deal more than we wished, but Fatima, who had travelled hundreds of miles with her former mistresses, Mesdames Hunter Blair, and Baker, was not to be thwarted, and she was right; she understood ruralising in India for better than we did.

With the exception of our large tin cases, we seemed to have left everything we generally used behind us, for we missed nothing upto the very moment of our departure; yet all must have been brought with us, for I, at least, never asked for a single article afterwards that was not forthcoming.

We drove to the Fort, on to the harbour, descended the broad steps of the ghaut, and entered a very good boat with a neat cabin in it sheltered by an awning. The sail down the coast of Malabar was very pretty, the blue sea under so brightly blue a sky, wooded shores, and a background of mountains. We had room enough to move about, for only the upper servants were with us, the rest, with the horses, the tents and other luggage, followed in our wake. Near sunset we reached Bancoote; it was a pleasure to climb up on our own feet, so seldom used in that country, a rather steep path to a half-ruined tower on a point of rock which was to be our resting-place for the night. The view from it was very fine, over land and sea and up a river which flowed swiftly round the rock.

We were still admiring it when called to dinner, and there, in the bare turret-room, was as neatly laid a table and as nice a small repast as any people need wish to sit down to. It had all been prepared on board the servants' bunder-boat. We had no roasts, but fish, stews, and curry, rice, fruit, and vegetables, all as well cooked as in the good kitchen at the Retreat. A saunter afterwards, and early to bed, my room as comfortable as in a warm climate was necessary, my own furniture in it, a shawl hung against the unshuttered window, and Fatima's little cot close to the door.

Colonel Smith had begged us to get over the bar at the mouth of the river with the morning tide, which served very early, and would help us on in our course up it; we were then to make no delay on leaving the boats but to push on up the mountain to a certain place—Mowlie, I think—where we were to pitch our tents for the night; but my father preferred his own plans. The boats got over the bar; as we had others which were within it, we went down to them in palanquins, and it was not a short trot; we had had our breakfast first comfortably in the ruined tower, after dressing leisurely, admiring the view, and gathering branches of oleander, almond, and other beautiful flowering shrubs.

It was all very pleasant in the cool of the morning, but the river was far from pleasant in the heat of the noon-day; part of the way it was confined by high banks, which reflected the sun's rays, and kept all air from us. We had not brought an awning, and the roof of the cabin soon heated through. It was three or four hours of suffering. On landing, my mother was so done up that the plan was again departed from, and instead of pushing on up the pass, we resolved to rest and dine at the spot we had been warned against at the foot of the mountain, a pretty little plain facing west, a rock rising behind and enclosing it, a hot wind blowing. It was a foretaste of what awaits the doomed! rest there was none. Every stitch of clothes but a gingham wrapper I threw off, tucked up the sleeves, opened the collar, pulled off my rings, took out my combs, which seemed to scorch my head, and, creeping below the table in my tent, lay there more dead than alive till the signal for moving was given; dinner was countermanded, a little fruit welcomed instead. When we were to march my palanquin was so hot I could not breathe in it; they threw *chatties* of water over it, and up rose a steam worse than the scorching.

We had to wait half an hour before I could bear its atmosphere.

At last we were off, and as the sun declined and the air cooled, and the ascending path brought the mountain air to us, I was able to look up and out, and enjoy the singular scene presented by our party.

A *barra sahib* needed a large retinue when travelling in the East years ago. First went Nasserwanjee on a *tattoo* (a little pony) leading us all, sword in hand, for the scabbard only hung by his side, the naked blade flourished at every turn above his head; next were some sepoys or peons, then my mother's palanquin and her spare bearers, then mine and more peons, then my father's, then the two ayahs'; next, the upper servants on ponies, but without swords; then under servants on foot or on bullocks; the luggage, tents, canteens, trunks, all on bullocks, peons and coolies running beside them to the number altogether of fifty or sixty. It was a long train winding round among the hills, always ascending and turning corners, and when night came on, and the torches were lit—one in about every fourth man's hand—the effect was beautiful, the flames waving as the arms moved, leaves, branches, rocks, gleaming in turn among the dusky train that wound along up the steep footway. Daylight might not have been so picturesque, but it would have been far more suitable to the kind of journey, and the distance being considerable, many a weary step was taken before we reached our resting-place.

It was near midnight when we came to three tents sent by General Robertson for our accommodation.

All we wanted was soon ready, for a fire was there, burning in a furnace made of stones, the usual travelling fireplace. Our curry was heated, I had nearly a whole bottle of beer, and my bed being ready by the time this supper was over, I was soon fast asleep in a region as wild as Glen Ennich.

My mother became quite reconciled next morning to our journey, for a messenger arrived very early with two notes for my father, one from General—then Colonel Robertson—and one from Colonel Smith; they were notes of welcome, with directions, which warned by the sufferings of the day before we obeyed; very kind they were—everybody is kind in India—but it was not the kindness that pleased my mother, it was the messenger! He was one of the irregular horse, a native, light made, handsomely dressed, in coloured trousers, flowing robe, and yellow cap (I think). He rode well and caracoled his little spirited horse before us for just as long as we pleased to look at him. She took it into her head that he was one of Colonel Smith's regiment—which regiment was Heaven knows where—in Gujerat, I believe—so she asked Nasserwanjee for a rupee to give him, and did the civil with the air of a princess.

After breakfast we started again; a long ascent, and then, just at dark, a stretch of level road, brought us to the end of our journey, a large double-poled tent of Colonel Smith's, which was to be lent to us during our stay on the hills. We had a very good dinner very well served, and retired to our sleeping-tents in great good-humour. The night was piercing cold, and the chill of the water next morning was really painful; but a canter warmed me and gave me also a good view of the curious place we were settled on, a wide plain on the top of a long ridge of mountains. The Governor's small bungalow, and the Resident's a little way off, were the only houses at the station; everybody else lived in tents, scattered about anywhere in groups of from five to six according to the size of the establishment.

The mountain air was enchanting, the sun hot in the middle of the day, yet quite bearable, the mornings and evenings delightful, the nights rather cold. The society was on the pleasantest footing; the way of life most agreeable as soon as we got into it. The first few days we kept our Bombay hours, late dinners, and so on, therefore an exchange of calls with our neighbours was the extent of our intercourse, but as soon as we showed ourselves well-bred enough to conform to the habits of the place we got on merrily: dined at the Robertsons often, lunched here and there, gave little dinners and little luncheons, and went with parties to the only two lions that there were, the sources of some river and a hill fort. We had Mrs. James Farquharson, and her sister Mrs. Simson; a fat man who amused us all, and a thin *padre* whom we must have amused, for he was always smiling; Sir Lionel Smith, and others.

One very disagreeable circumstance met us there, indeed accompanied us everywhere, my father's unfortunate dispute with the Government. It had begun some weeks before, and arose thus. Some native case, about Ramchander *somebody* (I might remember the name, for goodness knows how often I wrote it), which had been before the Sudder for a length of time, was removed into the Supreme Court, where the opinion of its three judges on its merits was in direct opposition to that of the Company's. Before my father's appointment, there had been serious misunderstandings between these two powers, each having been in some degree to blame. My father had been well "advised" by the Board of Control that it would be agreeable to have these differences healed, and that he could do nothing that would be better approved at home by both the Board of Control and the Court of Directors than to put an end to these unseemly jarrings. The Bombay Government, anxious to support their own authorities, were delighted at the new judge's connection with one of their own servants. Uncle Edward seized on my father at once, seconded by Mr. Norris, telling their own version of Sir Edward West's mistakes; but he, aided by the heavy weight of Sir Charles Chambers, got the upper hand of the Civil Service, and enlisted my father in right earnest on their own side. The Sudder Adawlut ordered one thing, the Supreme Court ordered another, the Governor in Council interfered, and the King's judges ignored the Government.

Mr. Norris, the only person whose advice my father might have listened to, had unluckily gone to the Neilgherries. Mr. Gardiner came to me one day—he was acting secretary then—to say that a most intemperate paper had been sent in by the three judges, and that as on some points they were decidedly in the wrong, serious disputes having grave results would be the consequence. I could not speak; he did without effect; I tried my mother, but she as usual was on the fighting side; so the quarrel spread till it became personal; all parties lost temper, all parties listened to tittle-tattle, and so it went on till both sides appealed to home.

At this point Sir Edward West died suddenly; his widow followed him in a week or so, leaving one orphan child, a little delicate girl, to the care of Sir Charles and Lady Chambers. In a month Sir Charles died also. Lady Chambers, poor woman, waited for her confinement — my mother and I standing godmothers to the posthumous child, Anne Catherine — and then sailed with all the orphans for England.

The overwork of the courts quite pleased my father, who went on capitally all his own way, as busy as half-a-dozen; but the Bombay Government interfering again about that Ramchander case, he, in a pet, closed the court, a step every one, including my mother, condemned; but he was thoroughly out of temper, and nobody to hold him in.

I forget whether he closed the court before or after our visit to Mahableishwar, but the dispute was in full vigour at that time, so we were out of the range of all the Governor's civilities, and never asked to meet him — that is, collectively. I individually was quite his friend, riding with him frequently in the mornings, at least till he fancied he might be in the way! He used to read me the letters he received from his wife and children, sent me newspapers, new books, flowers, etc.; and when it became known that I was soon to remove to Satara, he not only wished me joy with all his heart, and told me I was marrying one of the best fellows in the service, but he let me know that in the contemplated changes there would be no longer a brigadier at Satara, the Resident would command what troops were necessary, and that Colonel Smith would be removed. Where would I like to go to? Only once we got upon the quarrel; he said if I had been my father's wife instead of his daughter it would not have gone such lengths; so he had listened to gossip too.

I took very much to Colonel and Mrs. Robertson; he was delightful, quite a Scotchman, mostly self-educated. His innate goodness and long habits of authority had given him a commanding manner. He looked great at the head of his own long table, beaming his benevolent smiles all round. He read Burns aloud at some of our pleasant gatherings with the accent and the feeling of a countryman. Here, too, we made the better acquaintance of Major Jameson, son of old Bailie Jameson at Inverness, connected with the Alveses, Inglises, and other good northern bodies. Good-natured man! he used to devote hours to my mother gossiping with her over all the north *countrie*. She liked him better than any person in Bombay, and was certainly much happier after he came among us. He was not in my Colonel's regiment, but in another cavalry one, and wore the same handsome French grey uniform with silver. My Colonel used to meet me most mornings just where the path from our tents joined the road; we then went on together. One morning, either I was later than usual, or he was earlier, at any rate I arrived and he was not there. I did not know that I looked disappointed, but I suppose I looked up and down the road. "The Colonel Sahib has gone on," said the syce, pointing to the fresh marks of a horse's feet. I blushed, a little at the man's sharpness, a little at my cool Colonel's easy way of taking matters.

I had my coffee as usual after my ride, and then I often took a stroll round the tents, and then sat with a book near the curtain, which acted as door, looking out on the scene. Here I passed an hour or so before my father and mother joined me. She never rose early; he had almost given up his morning ride, not liking, perhaps, to meet the Governor. After breakfast we had our usual occupations, visitors or visiting, and then a neat toilette for an early dinner at home or elsewhere. In the evening a saunter, and I, often a drive in Colonel Smith's gig, none of us having brought up other carriages.

One day I had a ride on an elephant, an extremely disagreeable mode of travelling, like a boat heaving up the wrong way. The great beast knelt down, and I got up his side by the help of a little ladder slung to his back, and entered a curricle seat with a head to it. The roll of the creature as it rose was horrid, its walk ditto, and I was very glad to get safe on the ground again. Our strolls in the evening were checked by the appearance of a small green serpent, whose bite was venomous; a peon of the Robertsons' died in consequence, and as we did not know where they might be, their colour concealing them, we gave up our wanderings.

One day I was writing at a table near the door of the tent, my toes touching a pile of books on the ground beneath it. Nasserwanjee came behind, and laying one hand on my shoulder and the other on the back of the chair, he pulled back both together, asking pardon for the liberty; when I was at a safe distance two peons came forward and killed one of these little serpents, which had been lying close to the books and my toes. There's a pleasant interlude in one's occupations! I saw only one other strange animal in these mountains—a large monkey, or rather an ape, which I took for a little old Indian grown grey with age, for it was walking upright with a branch in its hand."—*Memoirs of a Highland Lady, pp. 434-440.*

3.

A Madras Military Officer on Mahabaleshwar.

A.D. 1835.

Adjutant L. advised me to go to Bombay viâ Mahabaleishwar hills, instead of by Poonah. His description of the festivities that were taking place on the hills, and the beauty of the scenery, speedily determined my choice.

Left Sattarah at midnight, and at day-light on the 17th May 1835 began to ascend the Ghauts, on my route to the hills. I was resolved to walk up them, in order to enjoy the beauty of the scenery; but I found it a more Herculean task than I had anticipated; the roads were zigzag and very bad, and the dust was very annoying. The scenery, however, amply recompensed for these inconveniences; towering mountains, whose summits seemed to be encircled by the clouds, while the bold peaks of others soared far above them, and proudly lifted up their heads into the region of ether; intricate labyrinths of trees shrouding them from the view; secluded solitary retreats, where the human foot had rarely or never been, and where fancy might paint the savage haunts of the prowling inhabitants of the forest. As I approached the summit [of Mahabaleshwar hills,] the air became quite cool and invigorating, and the eye was suddenly delighted with the animating spectacle of clusters of European bungalows overtopping the mountain ranges. I bent my course to a country seat, called Bohemia, the residence of the Hon. Mr. N—. I was agreeably surprised to find my kind host and a few friends at breakfast at so fashionable an hour as 11 a.m., which was occasioned by the prolonged festivities of a farewell ball given the preceding night by my Hon. friend, who was about to return to England with a handsome fortune. He was deservedly a great favourite both at Bombay and on the hills. After a residence of nearly thirty years in India, he still continued to be the life and soul of social intercourse; his departure will consequently be regretted by the *beau monde* in these parts.

I drove round the place to see the lions. The roads were good; the houses were built of stone, somewhat in the European style. The climate admitted of carpets, blankets, cloth waring-apparel, and a snug fire-side, etc. Hence, the hills have latterly been the general resort, as the sanitarium of the western districts of India, and will, no doubt, in a short time, entirely supersede the fatigue, danger, and expense of a long journey to the Neilgherry hills, which has hitherto been the plan adopted by invalids. The bungalows were situated in the midst of beautiful gardens, in which grew all sorts of fruits and vegetables: they in general occupy about ten to twenty acres of ground. In the neighbourhood, stands a pretty little English church. The mountain-fern, which is very uncommon in other parts of India, grows here in abundance. On a conspicuous part of a rising ground, an obelisk has been erected to the memory of Sir Sidney Beckwith.

At the period of my visit, there was a numerous party on the hills; a continued round of spirited convivialities formed a constant novelty and a striking contrast to the monotony and sickly indoor residence in the plains beneath. Here one may ride and walk all day long without inconvenience; and those who have a taste for the sports of the field may èngage in hunting the bison, which, however is attended with great risk and danger. A fine young man, cornet in H. M. 4th Dragoons, was lately killed by a bison, that burst upon him unawares from the midst of the jungle; he was several times spitted on its huge sharp horns and tossed into the air, and expired shortly after. His comrades had the poor satisfaction of subsequently killing the animal. Notwithstanding this unfortunate accident, they continue to pursue so dangerous a sport with as much avidity as ever. Wild cheetas and hyenas, too, are by no means uncommon. The first night of my stay at Mr. N.'s, a hyena entered the compound and came close up to my tent. Men, dogs and guns were hastily in requisition, but the animal escaped.

A grand bachelor's ball was in preparation, to which I had the honour of being appointed florist: the apartments were decorated with flowers and the verandah laid out with groves of orange and citron trees, and bowers of myrtle artificially cut and arranged; a large concourse of elegant ladies, however, formed by far the most charming portion of the ornaments. I could not help observing that the great majority of the ladies were unmarried, which is generally found to be the case amid the gay assemblages of Europeans in India. We had a strong muster of Portuguese musicians from Poonah who struck up quadrills, waltzes, Scotch reels, and country dances with great spirit. The coolness of the weather, combined with the spirit-stirring strings of the performers, soon lighted the beam in the eye and led on the festive dance. The supper was sumptuous, and (according to the phraseology of the gentlemen of the press) the wines gave general satisfaction.

I took my leave of the Mahableishwar hills with regret; and, after a stay of four days, resumed my journey on the 20th, at 4 P.M., accompanied by Mr. B. on horseback, one of the keenest and best sportsmen in India. He escorted me to the verge of the Ghauts, amid clouds of dust and showers of missile weapons discharged from the trees by the chattering monkies. A magnificent prospect of the sea now opened before me; the well-cultivated vales beneath smiled with waving crops of brightest verdure; a strong fort hung wildly on the brink of a frowning precipice, and lofty cliffs with their rugged heads rose far above the adjacent plain. The edges of the roads were frightfully abrupt; my head often became giddy while contemplating the profound abyss that yawned around. A false step of my bearers might have dashed us to atoms in an instant. We accomplished our descent, however, in safety, though by the timid and nervous it may fairly be considered a very hazardous undertaking, as there are other sources of danger quite as alarming as the apprehension of a broken neck. A friend of mine, during his progress upward, at midnight espied a cheeta asleep by the road side, quietly resting upon his paw; perceiving that it was unobserved by his bearers, who, if they had seen it, would have run off and left him exposed in a tonjon chair, he very prudently held his peace and was carried safely by, without waking his sleeping adversary.—*Asiatic Journal, 1836.*

4.

Mrs. Postans on Mahabaleshwar.

A.D. 1839.

* * * * * * *

The Dâk traveller, leaving Sattara in the evening, dawn sees him at the foot of the stupendous Ghauts, on which has been cut the road leading to the Mahabuleshwar Hills. Winding along the steep brows of lesser Ghauts, piled as it were to oppose the desecrating foot of man, the scene becomes rich in its features of sublime and fertile loveliness; each Ghaut being thickly wooded, from its pale purple and sunlit brow, to where the gathering and snowlike wreaths of fleecy clouds conceals its union with the Lowlands. On either side of the curving pathway, rich and graceful trees, festooned with a variety of blooming creepers, charm the eye; while about their knarled roots, as if hurled by the thunder-armed power of the giant storm, lie massive fragments of timestained rocks, crushing the verdure on which they fell, until time has again, with tenderest touch, encouraged fragile and flowery weeds to spring from their dark clefts, and sun their sweet heads in the passing breeze.

Continuing onwards, increased heights sink to insignificant effects; magnificent views increase in their glorious wonders; successions of towering mountains, varied and fantastic, bearing fresh and glowing verdure, here crowned with thin vapour, there resting on the azure sky in bold relief, fascinate the traveller's attention, until he attains the summit of the Mahabuleshwar Hills, and an atmosphere cold, clear, and most invigoratingly delightful.

The spot chosen for residence, is computed to be four thousand five hundred feet above the level of the sea. Pretty bungalows are erected, on eminences which command the most splendid combinations of scenery; and are interspersed with tents, the independent residences of many among the bachelor visitants to the Mahabuleshwar Hills. A Sanitarium affords comfortable accommodation to invalid officers, such persons being allowed the use of two apartments in it, at a monthly rent of twenty-five rupees. Near this spot, a simple obelisk has been raised to perpetuate the memory of Sir Sidney Beckwith, many years commander-in-chief of the Bombay Army. The domestic virtues of this amiable man, are eulogized in a few touching and appropriate lines, written by his widow.

The level ground of the Mahabuleshwar Hills, is covered with a tangled verdure, consisting principally of plants of fern and arrow-root, which latter has somewhat the appearance of a tall white lily, with large, smooth, and bright green leaves. The jungle abounds with tigers, buffaloe, neil ghye, bears, wolves, elk, and every description of game; but hunting in these wild solitudes, is often attended with great danger, and sometimes with fatal results. Sydney and Elphinstone Points, are immense bluffs of rock, from which the most extensive and magnificent views are obtained of the rich Concan scenery, and its beautiful fortresses, crowning the summits of surrounding Ghauts. The sea is visible at a distance of thirty miles; and the lovely gorges of the mountain-sides sparkle with innumerable cataracts, rushing with headlong violence to the placid streams, which wind among the rich pasturage of the sunny plains. About four miles from the Sanitarium, is the village of Mahabuleshwar, the source of the far-famed and very holy River Khrishna. The word Mahabuleshwar, in its divisions, signifies "the great and good God!" And over the sacred waters (which have two distinct sources) are large and curious temples, arched and columned, singular specimens of Hindoo architecture. In each, the stream issuing from the mouth of the Nandi, is received into a tank of inconsiderable size, whence it flows in a serpentine course through a beautiful and fertile valley, until, joined by the various waters which flow down the wooded gorges of the neighbouring hills, it swells into a rapid and scarcely fordable river. Few scenes are more lovely than the beautiful Valley of the Khrishna, as seen from the open Temples of Mahabuleshwar. The smooth and brightly gleaming waters, like a silvery thread, wind their quiet way between the richly wooded hills, which form a vista of fertile shelter to the grassy banks; while the herds, feeding peacefully beside the sacred river, complete the scene, and afford a glimpse of pastoral beauty, the more fair and sweet, perhaps, as contrasted with the sublime mountain solitudes of the immediate neighbourhood.

The necessary supplies of life, are readily procured upon the hills, from a good bazaar, stocked with European articles; the soil is highly favourable to cultivation, and several Chinamen possess gardens well stocked with English vegetables; the potatoes more particularly, being nearly equal to those of the Neilgherry hills; the beef and mutton are also of superior quality, the latter fine-grained, and of the most excellent flavour.

The climate of Mahabuleshwar is frequently sufficiently cold to render fires necessary, and is found highly renovating to constitutions exhausted by a long residence in the sultry plains. Fogs, in the autumn months, are prevalent, but are not found to produce either unpleasant or dangerous effects.

The walks and drives about the hills, are numerous and beautiful; long avenues, shaded by magnificent forest trees, afford noon-tide shelter, and permit the visitor the unusual and safe indulgence, of a mid-day stroll beneath their shade; while here and there an opening in the rich foliage, affords a glimpse of the superb mountain-scenery around, arresting the step in admiration of its sublime and varied wonders. Bold peaks, towering and cloud-capt Ghauts, sparkling cascades, hill-forts, deep straths, and wooded glens, blend their magnificent effects in a succession of rich and glowing pictures, more wondrous and more grand, than even Italy with her bold Alps and smiling Pyrenees can charm the traveller's eye withal. No snowy peaks, 'tis true, blushing in the rays of the sun-lit sky, form backgrounds to the scene; but veils of fleecy vapour, with mazy indistinctness, shroud the towering scarps of the eternal hills, while the clear atmosphere around, permits the eye to revel in the full majesty of these stupendous scenes, revealing the sun-lit valleys, and the quiet occupation of their peasants, as clearly as it does the dense jungle of the mountain side, crowded with its wild and savage denizens.

To the resident in Western India, the Mahabuleshwar hills are of incalculable value. They afford an invigorating retreat during the exhausting heat of the summer months; and the keen cold air of this delightful spot, re-strings the failing nerves, and plants fresh roses on the pallid cheek. The mind loses its presentiments of evil, and all the sad train of nervous and hypochondriac depressions, are over-powered by the new vigour of recovered health.—*Western India by Mrs. Postans, pp. 264-270.*

5.

Lady Falkland on Mahabaleshwar.

A.D. 1849.

* * * * *

Only those who have lived in the plains of India, can understand the feeling of an attenuated and exhausted European, the first day after his arrival at Mahabaleshwur—a very long word, which is, however, shorter when pronounced than when written, being usually called Mableshwur. The word signifies 'The Lord of great strength.' The latter syllable, 'eshwur,' being one of Siva's designations, and nearly equivalent to 'Lord,' as we use it in speaking of the Deity.

In the morning, when you wake, you think you have received a new set of bones: you get up refreshed, and your feet seem to run away with you.

The windows can be closed without your feeling it too warm, and open without feeling too cold. There are fire-places in the bungalows, and how often have I known people have a fire for the pleasure of seeing one, and in order to make them think that they were 'at home.'

Then a fog! when it *does* come (which is the case some times), how it is welcomed by many!— who say, "Oh, it reminds one of 'home!'" And I plead guilty to having gone out and stood in a shower purposely to receive the refreshing drops.

It is often possible to remain out till nine in the morning, when it is cloudy, and also to go out early in the afternoon.

The air is spring-like, light and crisp; when the slightest feeling of keenness arises, a soft breeze comes to your relief immediately.

Early in the morning—as is the case in all hilly countries—the mountains are partly covered with floating mists, that run along, visiting every rocky peak, which looks instantly cooled and refreshed.

The Mahabaleshwur Mountains are properly the Syhadree, deriving the former name from a small village about three miles from that part of the tableland where the European community reside.

If we may believe the true history of the Syhadree Hills at Mahabaleshwur, though now less than 5,000 feet high, they once reached to the skies; for the legend is: "That the sun used to find it very difficult to drive his day's journey in consequence of these hills, which used formerly to reach the skies, like the Himalayah. He sought counsel from Auguste Rishi, who was 'Gooroo,' or spiritual adviser, to the mountain. The holy man set out, and coming to the hills they of course bowed their heads before him. He said: "Stay there, my children, till I return," which he has never yet done; and hence the hills are still in the same position, lying in ridges along the plains of the Deccan; and the sun has never since had any difficulty in driving his chariot."

I always felt grateful to the gooroo for having lowered the hills, as it enabled us to see over their summits the beautiful sunsets, which are particularly fine.

These mountains are about 4,000 feet above the sea, which was visible in certain lights from a window of our bungalow, at the distance of thirty miles as the bird flies; and when the sun declined we could sometimes see little white specks on the distant ocean—they were ships; at other times the blue line of the water became a sheet of gold. This was the usual effect of the afternoon sun on it. Then there were lights and shadows for ever changing, throwing the sketcher who attempted to colour from nature, into the depths of despair.

The bungalows where the Europeans reside, are scattered about the table-land, and all are prettily placed and command lovely views.

The drives remind one very much of those in an English park; they are numerous, and have been well arranged. One missed the singing birds in the Concan, and here there were none; but we heard occasionally a few with wild abrupt notes, and saw soms with lovely plumage.

It will readily be believed that at the hills wild animals are not rare; cheetahs, or panthers, hyenas, and jackals, begin to prowl about at sunset; pet dogs are not unfrequently carried off by the panthers. Tigers, though by no means common, are occasionally 'marked down,' when the gentlemen go out on foot after them with beaters, sometimes to the number of a hundred, and the sportsmen are occasionally successful in bringing back a large royal tiger, or more frequently a cheetah. One year when we were at the hills, an acquaintance of mine was riding on one of the beautiful roads, when suddenly his horse stopped, and to his great surprise he saw a tiger descending a high bank into the road, it looked at the rider and horse for one minute, then slowly crossed over and disappeared in the jungle.

Snakes are more common than tigers. At the hills, there are long bright green ones: these often cling to the boughs of trees, and I have seen one dart down from a tree into the verandah of a bungalow, where two servants were sitting. It was soon killed. There is a small dark snake, called the carpet snake; it often enters houses, and being of the same colour as the mats, when lying on the floor, it is not always visible. I nearly trod on one once, under these circumstances.

Considering the number of these reptiles, it is astonishing how the natives, whose feet are only protected by slippers, escape being bitten. In our household, during a period of five years, one servant only was bitten; but he, poor fellow, died.

There is a tiny frog, known by the name of the flying frog; it has a singular power of jumping, and attaching itself to anything and everything. One of the creatures leaped up and fastened itself on the face of one of my maids. It was not pleasant, I admit, but there was something very ludicrous in it.

However, it is surprising how indifferent one becomes to frogs, snakes, cheetahs, hyenas, and tigers.

One evening, I was highly amused by a person coming to dine with us, exclaiming—"I have just killed a snake at the door!" Another guest followed saying—"The hyenas are howling dreadfully;" while a third came in and told us there had been a cry among his servants of 'baugh!' (tiger), in his compound.

When the hill season commences, the fact is soon made known by the quantities of furniture, which may be seen carried up the ghauts on men's heads. The bungalows are generally unfurnished; therefore visitors to the hills are obliged to send all they may require, and as the furniture has to go down the ghaut again in two or three months to prevent its being spoiled by the heavy rains, one can well imagine it is not in a very good condition at the end of the two journeys.

We often see a bath on one man's head; while another carries part of a bed, or a table; one has his head covered with a small tub; others carry a cane-bottomed sofa, and chairs, through which their heads are making an outlet, giving reason to fear the weary travellers will have very little to sit on when they arrive.

The roads above the ghauts are admirable, there are different points of views to which, in the evening, the visitors either drive or ride. One is Bombay-point, so called from its commanding the view of that part of the Ghaut, which the travellers ascend when they come from Bombay.

This is the finest of the many splendid views at the hills, and when I was in India, this was the point *par excellence*, where the society generally met in the evenings. Many came only to converse with their friends, and turning their backs on the view and sunset, were wholly occupied with the latest news, discussing whether Lieutenant this of the ——th Regiment, was really going to marry Miss——, if Mr.——was going home on 'sick leave,' and who would do his duty, the odd appearance Captain ——presented with his head shaved after his fever, or the report that a cheetah had carried off Mrs.——'s pet dog on the evening before.

The sunsets viewed from Bombay point are magnificent. We look over masses of trees, and mountain after mountain receding into a middle distance, where Pertabghur rises in the deepest possible shadow at this time of day.

On its summit the trace of walls and temples can just be made out. But there is still much beyond Pertabghur, for we see ranges of retiring mountains, seeming to touch the dark-blue line of the horizon. This is the ocean, and just above it is a ball of fire about to disappear into that dark-blue line. When the sun is gone we often see it reflected for a minute in the sea.

Every evening there was a different sunset; all beautiful, except when the sun looked 'bilious' and 'out of sorts,' as it frequently does in England. Then the dark grey clouds looked cross too, and soon shut it out from our view.

Among these mountains there is the wildest scenery that can be imagined, and spots where no human foot can ever have trod. It was always a strange feeling to me to look down on those wild solitudes, so completely inaccessible even to the children of the soil, who never could have set their feet among the dense jungle, nor climbed up the perpendicular sides of the abrupt surrounding mountains, among which wander bisons, tigers, cheetahs, hyenas, small-deer, jackals and monkeys.

New points commanding glorious prospects are often discovered, to which narrow paths are cut in the jungle. The sides of such a path form high tapestry walls of long reeds, grass, rushes, and ferns entwined with wild flowers, while overhead, the trees with their boughs and leaves form a ceiling of net-work. One such point was discovered the last time I was at the hills. I saw it for the first time at sunset when the most delicately tinted little rosy clouds were floating on the soft greyish-blue sky.

Below us were ravines and rocky precipices, where we watched the shadows falling lower and lower till seemingly lost in fathomless depths, where even the rays of the Indian sun could scarcely penetrate. In the distance were countless ranges of mountains almost the same colour as the sky, with the high lights here and there on their rocky peaks of a similar rosy tint to that of the clouds.

Nearer to us, mountains, thrown up in the strangest form, stood out in bold relief—some appearing to have been suddenly raised, and almost looking as if 'rearing up;' others, that seemed to have been torn asunder, stood as isolated pyramids; others, again, appeared to have been cut into square blocks; and from some of the more conical shaped ones, it was almost disappointing not to see smoke and flames rising up into the blue sky.

The fore-ground was all an artist could desire: it was beautifully broken, with masses of rock embedded among tall, waving fern, and low, thorny bushes, underneath which little humble wild-flowers seemed to have retreated and taken shelter. Then there were lofty trees, with straggling roots, and with either great mossy trunks and boughs, or with slender stems, having tints of grey, red, and yellow on them, all blending into each other; and close by was a cactus-looking tree, rising out of brambles, gigantic reeds, and the enormous leaves of the *circuma cauhina.* But numerous as are such scenes for those who like a solitary walk in the woods, the fashionable promenades and drives are equally so, and much more frequented. There are to be met the same people every evening.

On approaching the different points, one knows Mrs.——is at hand, for her gorahwallahs wear green-and-gold puggrees (turbans).

Then there are at few ladies of the *crême dè la crême,* who like to dash along in their carriages, disturbing the red dust of the road, which covers all their neighbours; and the gorahwallahs have to jump down at every turn to see if anything is in the way.

The number of attendants on the English children must astonish all new-comers from Europe. During the evening drive, one sees, at some little distance, a long train of people advancing at a slow pace. What can it be? Is it the body of the Hindoo carried forth to be burnt, or a religious procession?

As they come near we see women in white, natives with parasols, then ponies, and soon perceive, among the crowd, some little children: they are taking their evening airing. The women in white are the ayahs: they wear white sarees, gold bangles, and nose-rings; one carries a pale-faced 'chotah butcha' (little child), 'in long petticoats,' and over the infant's head a native man-servant holds a parasol; then comes a small carriage, drawn by a man and in it sits another child. The procession ends with a pony, on which is a little boy; he is held on by one attendant, while another leads the animal: both the young charioteer and rider are protected from the evening sun by servants carrying parasols, and thus they all creep on for an hour every evening at the same funereal pace.

* * * * *

It is scarcely safe to remain at the Mahabaleshwur Hills after the first week of June. The rains are then very frequent; the roads, up and down the Ghaut, are nearly impassable, and the rivers not always fordable. Bridges are not common, and the traveller, either in his carriage or palanquin, has frequently to wait some time till it is safe to pass over the rivers. Visitors at the hills therefore hurry back either to Bombay or Poonah at the beginning of June. As soon as they leave, those in charge of the bungalows prepare for three months and a half of continual rain. It is a rain of which no one who has not been in India can form an idea. In the three months and a half, upwards of three hundred inches of rain generally fall at the hills; and the fall has been known to exceed three hundred and fifty.

I have only heard of one person, not a native, passing many monsoons at the hills, and that person was the widow of an American missionary. There she lived for several years, having, in the rainy season, no one with her but a few native servants; snakes, hyenas, tigers, land-crabs, and cheetahs, her only neighbours.

The first preparation for this deluge is the packing up of the bungalows. Each is completely encased in a most comfortable great-coat, consisting of 'chuppers,' which are large screens of thatch, fastened to frames of poles, and so contrived that they cover up each face of the cottage, and prevent the rain from reaching the walls.

The chimney is taken care of in the same manner; the bungalow has no longer any shape whatever; it looks much like the figures of ladies in the loose "polka" great-coat, which has been the fashion of late years, and is more useful than graceful. The only inmate of the bungalow in the rains, is the 'mali' (gardener), who, I hear, when once he enters, never leaves it again till the fine weather re-appears, except to get the necessaries of life; he lays in a store of provisions and comforts, rice, ghee, cocoanuts, barley, tobacco, and fire-wood.

On the morning when we left the hills it was raining very much, and a storm seemed likely to follow,

> " There, like a string of elephants, the clouds,
> In regular file, by lightning fillets bound,
> Move slowly at their potent god's command;
> The heavens let down a silver chain to earth;
> The earth that shines with buds and sheds sweet odours,
> Is pierced with showers, like diamond-shafted darts.
> Launched from the rolling mass of deepest blue,
> Which heaves before the breeze and foams with flame,
> Like ocean's dark waves by the tempest driven,
> And tossing high their flashing surge to shore."

—*Lady Falkland's Chow-Chow, p.p. 142-153 and 183-185.*

6.

Author of the "Life in Bombay" on Mahabaleshwar.

A. D. 1853.

* * * * *

The season is over, and, as March approaches, the retired votary of pleasure, and the drooping invalid, are reminded by the increasing heat to seek for a renovation of health and spirits by an excursion to the Mahabuleshwur hills, the most favourite sanitary station of this side of India. At this season of the year the trip is easily and expeditiously effected, by proceeding per steamer down the coast as far as Bancoot, a distance of about seventy miles, and thence in a bunder-boat up the pretty Sawitree river to Mhar, thirty miles further. This is a large native town, conveniently situated on the banks of the river, but so hot, dirty, and disagreeable, that no one would willingly remain a moment beyond the time necessary for refreshment, and arrangements for the twenty-seven miles of land journey still to be accomplished.

Here was our first experience of a traveller's bungalow, which, though in our total ignorance, we then looked upon with the utmost contempt, we have since learnt to prize as an inestimable comfort in the otherwise shelterless journeys of India. These buildings are erected by Government for the accommodation of travellers, and generally contain from two to four rooms, scantily provided with the barest necessaries of furniture, and, excepting on well-frequented roads, often possessing no mess-man or (landlord) to minister to the wants of the hungry visitants. These things are, however, well understood, and a considerable portion of foresight and providence is speedily acquired under circumstances where necessity has no law, and the traveller must either make a proper provision for his journey, or starve.

The little expedition to Mahabuleshwur is now so smooth and straightforward, that the stranger is almost disappointed at the perfect ease with which it is performed, and at the absence of everything approaching to an adventure in the beautiful tract of country between Mhar and Kaneishwar, a village situated at the foot of the Ghâts. Even the shadowy romance attached to one's pre-conceived notions of mid-night palanquin travelling, surrounded by numerous bearers, scaring with their flashing torches the prowling tiger, fiercely glaring from the adjacent jungle, was quickly dispelled as we stepped into a comfortable public conveyance, called a stage-phaeton, and jogged along with a degree of homely safety and certainty totally incompatible with the former high-flown ideas of eastern pomp, and eastern perils, until we approached the foot of the Ghâts, where it became necessary to exchange the phaeton for a palanquin, in order to accomplish the precipitous ascent in comfort and security.

The grandeur of the scenery is beyond description, as we wind up this magnificent chain of mountains, which rise abruptly from the flat Concan, to an elevation of four thousand seven hundred feet above the level of the sea; the whole clothed in the richest verdure, and presenting at every turn of the path some new and startling feature of beauty, from the towering peak, with its summit concealed in the clouds, to the gushing waterfall, bounding and sparkling like sunbeams through the clefted rocks, until it finds itself a bed in the placid river which flows beneath.

Day was just breaking as we commenced the ascent, and never before did we experience so vivid a perception, so perfect a realisation of these exquisite lines.

"Night wanes—the vapours around the mountins curl'd
Melt into morn, and light awakes the world."

The clouds slowly unwreathed themselves from the heights they had encircled during the past night, and appeared to roll downwards with majestic reluctance, as if in obedience to the imperative summons of the approaching god of day. The scene was grand, and the effect upon the mind almost overpowering; but soon this feeling of exultation subsided into an extreme exhilaration of the animal spirits, as involuntary as though we had swallowed a tolerable dose of laughing-gas, and recklessly bid defiance to the grovelling cares of the world below. This, we afterwards learnt, is a very common effect attendant upon a first view of such magnificent scenery, in conjunction with inhaling the highly-rarified air of these stupendous mountain heights; and though this great excitability naturally abates as the eye becomes accustomed to the grandeur which surrounds it, there remains a degree of elevation of spirit, and consequent increased energy of mind and body, which greatly add to the enjoyment and benefit of a trip to "the hills."

The ascent of the Ghât occupies about four or five hours, and on reaching the table-land at the top, we were greeted by the sight of well-made roads, neatly thatched bungalows, picturesquely distributed over a space of several miles, and in short, of every evidence of civilised life and comfort, which English enterprise, and English wealth can cause to spring into life, even though located between four and five thousand feet above the level of the sea.

Strange to say, we have no authentic account of the first discovery of these hills. The earliest information that exists regarding them is, that they were visited by Colonel Lodwick in the hot season of 1824, at a considerable personal risk, from the vast numbers of tigers, bears, and cheetas, which infested these unexplored regions; and, notwithstanding his report of the wonders of the climate and scenery, the obstacles and dangers were considered so insurmountable, that no steps were taken to establish a station until the year 1828, when the present one was founded by Sir John Malcolm, then Governor of Bombay, and named by the Rajah of Sattara in honour of him, Malcolm Peth.

The derivation of the word Mahabuleshwur, is supposed to be from the three Mahratta words, "Maha," "bul," and "eeshwur," which signify "the God of great power," bearing that poetical adaptation to the circumstances of the case, which invariably characterises the Oriental phraseology. But who can behold the glories of the varied scene, which the eye takes in almost at a single glance, the countless mountains, as yet untrodden by the foot of man; the deep, gloomy ravines, unfathomable but by the beast of prey; the cliffs, which rise in naked majesty, proudly surveying the thunder clouds as they form, and burst beneath them; who, we ask, can look upon this scene of awful beauty, and not feel in his inmost heart, that He who created it is "the God of great power?"

Mahabuleshwur, properly so called, is a Brahminical village, situated about three miles from the English station of Malcolm Peth, though on the same line of table-land. It possesses a temple dedicated to the God Mahodeo, of considerable architectural beauty, and great reputed sanctity, being erected on the spot, whence the Holy Krishna takes its source. A smaller temple stands on the brink of a precipice, fringed with the bristling milk bush, and overlooking the valley through which the infant stream pursues its thread-like course; perceptibly widening, however, as contributions from the mountain rivulets gush freely in, until at length, swollen into a noble river, it sweeps proudly down the opposing Ghât, receiving throughout its farspread progress, the universal homage of the idolatrous Hindoos.

The village of Mahabuleshwur is on the high road to Elphinstone Point, one of the principal objects of attraction to every one who visits the hills. It is a cliff of immense height, with the point projecting considerably beyond the base, so that the eve of the spectator looks direct down a fall of three thousand feet, into the valleys of the Concan below! This view struck us as being too terrific to be pleasing; there is a greater appearance of monotony in the comparatively pigmy undulations of the surrounding eminences, than in any other part of the hills; and it appeared to us, that the much talked-of wonders of Elphinstone Point showed to greater advantage on being looked at from a distance, than on being looked from.

The oldest English residence of this station is Mount Charlotte, built by Sir John Malcolm, and thus named in honour of his daughter. It is said to stand upon the highest inhabited point of the hills, though the neighbouring elevation of Mount Malcolm rises to an elevation of nearly two hundred feet above it. This lovely spot is now the property of the venerable Bishop of Bombay, who previous to his departure for England, here made his highland home during a portion of every year, and greatly improved its many natural advantages by the addition of a large garden and cultivated grounds.

The terrace which surrounds the house commands one of the most extensive views of the station, embracing in the distance Muckrunghur (commonly called from its appearance, the Saddle Hill), and a continuation of Ghát scenery, varied and grotesque in outline extending beyond the reach of any human eye. But the nearer prospect is one of extreme and softened loveliness, including some of the most tastefully situated bungalows on the hills; and conspicuous amongst them, supported by its shining white pillars, stands Glen Ogle, appearing like a fairy bower in a garden of beauty, Bohemia, the usual residence of the Governor, or Commander-in-chief, built upon a mere shelf of rock overhanging a deep ravine; and Mount Douglas, whose dark-thatched roof forms the crowning point of the wooded height from which it peeps.

The principal public buildings of interest consist of, first, the neat little church, built by private subscription some years ago, and capable of containing about one hundred and eighty people; a sanitarium for the reception of sick officers; and a tolerably well furnished circulating library, a great desideratum in a place where relaxation is the order of the day, and where consequently all that contributes to render the "dolce far niente" life more agreeable is eagerly seized upon.

In the centre of the station and close to the church, a monument has been erected to the memory of Sir Sidney Beckwith, who, as Commander-in-chief and senior member of council, temporarily succeeded Sir John Malcolm, as Governor of Bombay in 1830, and died here the following year. The colour of the soil at Mahabuleshwur adds much to the general effect of the landscape. It is of a vivid red, and is a description of clay, formed by the union of a disintegrated ferruginous clay stone, with "débris" of trap rock; and in places where considerable portions of decayed vegetable matter are intermixed, a most fertile mould is produced, bearing spontaneously a profusion of brilliant coloured flowers, and an abundant supply of the pretty white of blossomed curcuma, from the root of which an excellent kind of arrowroot is obtained. But what most tends to gladden the heart of the English resident, is to find large tracts of country literally covered with the beautiful fern, (pteris aduillina) never met with in these latitudes below a certain elevation; and who can wonder if its feathery, branch-like leaves, are welcomed with rapturous emotions, as emblems of the home we may never see again!

Some industrious Chinamen have settled upon these hills, and contrive to make a comfortable livelihood by the cultivation of large gardens, producing abundance of excellent potatoes, and almost every description of European fruits and vegetables, which thrive in this climate surpassingly well even now, and in the course of a few years, will doubtless be brought to full perfection.

Towards the north side of the station, the landscape assumes a more barren and uninteresting appearance, which has been happily improved by the formation of an artificial lake, extending upwards of a mile in length, and constructed by the late Rajah of Sattara. This not only secures a large and unfailing supply of water for the purposes of cultivation, but has induced the construction of a variety of agreeable drives, and bridle paths, leading to many points of interest, which might otherwise have remained undiscovered.

A very popular excursion for a pic-nic party, or social drive, is to Kate's Point, a remarkable looking rock about four miles from the church, and approached by a pretty road winding down to the margin of the lake, from whence it diverges into rough and broken paths, over which we scrambled as best we could, trusting to the sure footing of our tattoos, or country ponies. This singular cliff at first sight, gives one the idea of a gigantic needle's head, so large is the perforation admitting a distinct view of the mountain ridges behind it. It forms a natural tunnel under the point, which rises perpendicularly on one side, over the valley of the Whye, and falls gradually on the other, into platforms of the rock, which render it perfectly accessible to the foot of man. The most striking feature in the scenery, after the point itself, is the fluted appearance of the mountain's sides, occasioned by the torrents of rain perpetually rushing down during the monsoon, which unimpeded in their progress by a single tree, form innumerable channels, crossing and intersecting each other like the veins of a leaf, and all contributing to swell the infant streams of the three rivers, which have their source in this valley. We allude to the Kristna or Krishna, the Yena, and the Keyna, which all take their course towards the Deccan; besides these, two other rivers rise amid the hills of Mahabuleshwur, the Sawitree, and the Gawitree; which taking an opposite direction, flow over the western side of the Ghât, to fertilize with their waters the lowlands of the Concan.

The amount of rain which falls here during the monsoon months, bears a great disproportion to that of the surrounding country, and renders the place uninhabitable even to the natives. It is completely enveloped in mist and cloud, which do not disperse until some time after the weather has cleared up in the lower regions; and those imprudent people who rashly visit the hills early in October, have not unfrequently to encounter all the miseries of finding their bungalows thoroughly saturated with damp. Indeed, we have known instances where the occupants have been obliged to walk about the house armed with umbrellas and clogs, whilst the floors of the different apartments presented the extraordinary spectacle of being covered by tubs and every description of vessel to receive the rain, steadily pattering, quite at its ease, through the roof, which acted as a sieve.

It is calculated that the number of days on which rain falls at Mahabuleshwur is one hundred and twenty-seven, the average amount being two hundred and twenty-nine inches, whilst that of Bombay is only seventy-five; and in Poona, and indeed throughout the Deccan, a fall of nineteen inches is considered a very fair and favourable monsoon, quite sufficient to ensure a healthy season, and to answer all agricultural purposes. The mean annual temperature of the station is said to be 66°; during the rainy season 63° 8′, and even in the very height of the hot weather, it seldom exceeds 72°, at the same time that in the country below, and within a few hours' ride of the hills, the thermometer stands at 110°.

The blessing of possessing such an accessible place of resort is incalculable; and many a painful separation in domestic life has been averted, in cases where the failing health of a delicate wife, or drooping child would have elicited the imperative medical order of a voyage to England, had not the happy resource of a trip to the hills existed.

One of the most crying evils of an Indian life is the necessity entailed upon parents of parting from their offspring at so tender an age, that the heart is wrung with agony at the bare idea of committing them to the charge of strangers; but this is unavoidable, not only as regards health, but education. In most children the constitution, after six or seven years of age, becomes visibly enfeebled, and the general lassitude which pervades the system renders an application to study almost impracticable, and warns the parents that it is time for their treasures to depart.

It has often struck us, with reference to these little creatures, that although everywhere engaging, they are here peculiarly objects of passionate love, whether from the consciousness that they must so soon disappear, or that they are actually more attractive from the circumstances which are inevitable in an Indian household. Unshackled by the discipline of an English nursery, and the tyranny of a head nurse, both of which tend to engender a spirit of reserve and even cunning, they roam at will through every part of the house, prattling with all the artlessness of fearless childhood, and effectually twining themselves round the affections of every member of the family, and visitor to the house; whilst to the native servants they are objects of positive idolatry. Great care and watchfulness are requisite on the part of a mother, to prevent the evil effects which might result from the overwhelming indulgence which the Ayahs especially are too apt to bestow upon their little charges.

* * * * *

In a place so greatly abounding with picturesque scenery, as Mahabuleshwur, it becomes almost impossible to particularise the many objects of interest which tempt the enterprising visitors to constant exertion, and induce a general spirit of sociability in the arrangement of pic-nic parties, riding and sporting excursion. We must not, however, omit to mention in our catalogue of remarkable spots, the beautiful elevation called Sidney Point situated about two miles from the church, and commanding an imposing view of Elphinstone Point and the Concan on one side, whilst on the other it looks down abruptly upon the lovely vale of Clifton, thickly studded with pretty bungalows, and presenting a scene so calm and homelike, as it lies in its quiet beauty, guarded by lofty encircling cliffs as may well suggest a train of thought the very reverse of that, so lately aroused by the contemplation of the wild grandeur of the opposite side. It is in the valley of Clifton principally, that several bungalows have been erected by Government for the accommodation of sick officers and their families; thereby ensuring a greater degree of comfort and privacy, than could be obtained at the sanitarium, and at a rent sufficiently moderate to come within the means of a married subaltern.

These dwellings are placed under the control of the medical officer, who acts as general superintendant of the station, residing here entirely from October to June, and at Sattara, or Poona, during the four months of the monsoon. Upon the energy and activity of this officer depends much of the enjoyment to be experienced in a visit to the hills. His multifarious duties comprise those of a magistrate, post-master, doctor and indeed universal referee to the entire of the inhabitants; with him rests the important arrangements for dák travelling, and the employment of the Chinese convicts confined in the jail, whose services have been turned to considerable account of late years, in the formation of excellent carriage roads, and bridle paths, which, intersting the station for an extent of nearly fifty miles, throw open every point of interest in the varied scenery of the hills.

Amongst these, one conspicuously worth of notice, and selected by general consent as a place of rendezvous, during the evening drive, is a spot situated at the top of the Ghát on the Concan side, and known by the name of Bombay Point. The grand feature of this scene is the perfect view it presents of the mountain fortress of Purtabghur, which formed part of the Sattara territory, and was a favourite occasional residence of the late Rajah up to the time of his death.—*" Life in Bombay," p.p. 67-83 and 87-89.*

APPENDIX I.

OBSERVATION ON THE CLIMATE OF THE MAHABULESHWUR HILLS,

(BY DR. JAMES MURRAY.)

Topography.

The Mahabuleshwur Hills form part of that extensive chain of mountains known under the name of the Western Ghats, which stretch from the province of Candeish to Cape Comorin, in a line nearly parallel with the coast. They take their name from the small Brahmin village of Mahabuleshwur, which is situated at the northern extremity of the table land, and is of reputed sanctity from its position at the source of the "holy Kristna." Their situation in relation to the circumjacent country, may be considered to be in a great measure insulated. The narrow valley of the Kristna forms their northern boundary, and leaves only a narrow neck of land to connect them with the general range in that quarter, and at their southern extremity the hill takes a sudden bend to the south-east, and narrows to a considerable extent their continuity with the southern part of the chain. On their western side they rise with an abrupt and precipitous ascent from the Concan, which separates them from the sea by a belt of land, from twenty-five to thirty miles in breadth; while their eastern face presents a somewhat less rapid and steep descent into the table land of the Deccan. Though the boundaries of the station are thus strongly marked, and distinctly defined, it varies considerably as to length and breadth, in consequence of lateral ramifications, which branch off at different points. Its greatest breadth at the northern extremity is about fifteen miles, and about eight at its southern boundary. The average direct length North and South does not exceed five miles, though from N. E. to S. W. it extends diagonally seventeen miles.

The site selected for the position of the sanatarium is in 17° 56′ North latitude, and in longitude 73° 30′ East, being distant twenty-five miles due East from the sea, and sixty-nine miles direct distance from Bombay, which bears No. 29°. W. The situation is a favorable one on the seaward, or western slope near the edge of the mountain, and is consequently freely exposed to the influence of the sea breezes, while it is to a certain extent protected against the force of the easterly winds. On the spot, also, has arisen a new village, which the Rajah of Sattara (to whom it originally belonged) appropriately named *Malcolm Peth*, in honor of the late Sir John Malcolm, the distinguished founder of the station.

The general elevation of the station has been ascertained, by a series of barometrical observations conducted by Mr. Walker, to be 4,500 feet above the level of the sea, while its highest summit attains an altitude of 4,700 feet. It is elevated upwards of 4,000 feet above the subjacent country on the Concan side, and more than 2,000 feet above the level of the Deccan, at its eastern base. The surface of the station is generally undulating, and in some parts hilly; but it is in many places practicable for wheeled carriages.

The soil consists principally of a red clay, formed by the disintegration of the cellular ferruginous clay stone, which here constitutes the surface rock, and overlies the secondary trap formation. This rock occurs, most generally, in superficial or detached masses, whose outer surface becomes hardened, and blackened by oxidation from exposure to the air. When first quarried it is comparatively soft, and of a brick-red colour, intermixed with lighter coloured streaks. From the facility with which it is hewn, and from its quality of hardening by exposure, it forms an excellent and cheap material for building purposes: but, from its cellular structure, requires to be protected by *tatties* during the rainy season. It contains a considerable impregnation of iron, and is advantageously smelted for that purpose.

The laterite soil formed from this rock, though scanty on the summits of the rising grounds, is, in the lower levels, intermixed with the debris of trap rock, and in some places with a considerable proportion of decayed vegetable matter, forming a brown mould, which is found to be abundantly productive. The soil, after a few days exposure to heavy rain, becomes tenacious, and this allows a great proportion of the subsequent water to run off; an effect which is greatly promoted by the undulating nature of the ground. It never at any time becomes muddy; nor is there any where on the hill the slightest appearance of a swamp or marsh.

An abundant supply of excellent water is at all seasons procurable either from wells, or from the small streamlets, which traverse the hills in various directions, several of which retain their water during the whole of the hot season. It is generally to be reached by digging to a depth of from ten to forty feet.

Very little cultivation exists as yet at this station, there being only a few small patches of ploughed ground, on which are grown the common grains of the Deccan. Within the last two years, however, there has been a very considerable increase of the cultivation of potatoes, which are found to be of finer quality than any that have been produced elsewhere in Western India. A plentiful supply of all the common culinary vegetables of the best description can be procured at reasonable rates.

Botany.

The general absence of forest trees gives, at first sight, an appearance of bareness to the table land of the hills. A few groups and avenues of fine trees decorate some portions of the main road, the line of which they follow with so much regularity as to convey the impression of their having been planted for the express purpose of shade and ornament. They consist principally of the *Calyptranthes caryophyllifolia* (Jambool), by far the commonest tree all over the table land ; the *Memecylon ramiflorum* (Arjun), which looks very beautiful at all seasons, with its small polished dark green leaves, but particularly so from February till April, when its numerous blue and purple flowers appear through the foliage, clustering round the naked branches; the Peesah, a species of *Tetranthera*, flowering in November, and bearing a small acorn looking berry, half enclosed in the calyx, and contrasting strongly in its light coloured foliage with all the other trees; the *Olea dioica*, (Par. Jamb.), the *Terminalia chebula* (Heerda), the *Symplocos racemosa*, an erect growing tree with large leaves of a thick, firm texture, and almond-scented flowers; and the *Ficus glomerata* (Oomber) or water tree of the Natives, growing almost to as large a size as it does in the low rich lands of the Concan.

Of the rarer trees and shrubs may be mentioned, *Figara triphylla*, hitherto not noticed by any botanist as a native of the Peninsula, the *Pittosporum floribundum*, the *Eriochlena Hookeriana*, *Pygeum acuminatum*; a *Salix*, perhaps the *tetrasperma* of Roxburgh, a species of *Elaeocarpus*, *Urtica pulcherrima Rubus ru gosus*, and *Cupia thyrsoides*.

In addition to those already enumerated may be noticed the *Pentaptera tomentosa* (Ain). and *Paniculata* (Keenjora), a species of *Conocarpus* (Daura), the Mango tree, some species of *Bignonia* and *Bauhinia*, the *Briedelia montana* (Asana), &c. These are chiefly to be found in ravines and sheltered situations on the western face of the Hills.

The copse which in some parts is very thick, consists of the *Gardenia montana* (Ghela). It attains a considerable size in sheltered situations, but is generally found in the form of a scraggy bush. Its pale yellow flowers begin to appear in April, and possess, like most of the family, a considerable fragrance. The fruit much resembles a crab apple, and hangs on the bushes till the flowering time of the succeeding year—the *Baeobotrys indica* (Atkee), the *Solanum giganteum* (Chunna), the *Eleagnus conferta* (Amgool), *Colebrookia ternifolia* (Bhamnee), *Flacourtia sepiaria* (Tamboot), the *Callicarpa lanata* (Eisur), *Pavetta indica* (Paput), *Scutia indica* (Chimtee), *Ziziphus rugosa* (Toorun), *Limonia monophylla*, a species of *Celastrus* (Yenkul), a shrub called *kala goora*, the *Karwah*, so commonly used in wattled buildings, a species of *Bradleia* called *Bhoma* by the Natives, and an *Osyris* (Lotul).

Of climbing plants may be noticed the *Arbut*, figured by Rheede in the Hortus Malabericus under the name of *Pu-Valli*, but which does not yet appear to have found its way into any systematic work. It flowers in December and is very common—the *Embilia robusta* (Karkunie), *Josminum latifolium* (koosur), and *Hoya viridiflora*.

With the exception of the *Karwah* and *Gardenia*, none of the above are at all remarkable for the beauty of their flowers. The only truly ornamental shrubs are the *Gnidia eriocephala* (Rameta), and the Dingala, a species of *Crotularia*. Both are very common and add greatly to the beauty of the landscape when in flower; the latter particularly, covered with its abundant light yellow blossoms, presents at a distance a considerable resemblance to the "long yellow broom." A shrubby species of *Indigofera*, called Neerda, also deserves to be put in this class, and the *Clematis gouriana*, and *grata*.

The most striking feature in the vegetation, is the profusion of the common Brake, *Pteris aquilina.* It is most abundant every where, rises in some places to the height of nine or ten feet, and serves to recall the endearing associations of a more northern clime. A very beautiful species of *Osmunda* abounds in the vale of the Yena and other damp situations.

A considerable number and variety of annual and other plants spring up in succession during the greater part of the year. Of these a species of *Carcuma,* probably the *montana* of Roxburgh appears in the greatest abundance every where, at the commencement of the rains. From its roots, an excellent description of Arrow root is procured. The beautiful *Amaryllis insignis*, the snake lily (a species of *Arum*), the *Curculigo brevifolia, Exacum bicolor, Plader avirgata*, a skecies of *Phlomis*, and a plant with yellow flowers resembling a *Conyza*, are also common.

There is a considerable variety of parasitic *Orchidiæ* some of which possess great beauty. Two or three species of *Loranthus*, the *Vicum Wighteanum*, and *compressum* (Indian Misletoe), and *Cuscuta reflexa* are also commonly met with.

The trunks and branches of many of the trees are covered with a variety of *Lichens* and *Musci*, and as the botany of the hills has only been partially and imperfectly examined, it is probable some of them may be new to science.

Climate.

In tracing the physical characters of the climate through the different months, it will be convenient to divide the year into three seasons, the *cold*, the *hot*, and the *rainy* seasons. As the transition from one season to another is generally gradual, and their respective duration varies somewhat in different years, it is impossible to define the precise limits of each with perfect accuracy. Instead of adopting the more uniform and customary division into three seasons of four months each, (a division which generally holds good on the plains,) it will comport better with the usual distribution of temperature here, to assign five months to the *cold*, three months to the *hot*, and four months to the *rainy* season. Under this arrangement, the cold season will embrace the months of October, November, December, January, and February; the hot season will include March, April and May; and the rainy season will comprise the remaining months of June, July, August, and September.

The remarks which follow are founded on a series of meteorological registers which have been carried on without interruption for eight consecutive years, and form an aggregate of upwards of ten thousand thermometrical observations. The mean results of temperature are deduced from observations made at the two periods of greatest cold and heat. The hours when these two daily extremes are indicated will be more particularly noticed hereafter. The temperatures are taken from thermometers suspended out of doors in a verandah which is protected from the direct Influence of the solar rays by a thatched roof, but is freely exposed to the open air on the northern side, without the intervention of venetian or other screen. The degree of atmospheric humidity has been ascertained by wrapping the bulb and lower part of the stem of a thermometer in muslin, and, having wetted the covered bulb with spring water, by observing (as compared with a dry naked thermometer placed side by side in the shade) the amount of depression arising from the cold produced by evaporation. These hygrometrical observations have only been recorded for two years.

The commencement of October may be considered as the connecting link between the rainy and cold seasons. The weather during this month combines the good qualities of the climate of both seasons, and is altogether the most genial and pleasant throughout the year. The temperature is cool and equable, and there is an agreeable freshness in the air, which is not experienced in the same degree at any other period. It reminds the visitor of an European spring, and forms a pleasing and striking contrast with the oppressive weather experienced at this period on the plains, and more especially on the coast. During the early part of the month, there is an agreeable alternation of cloud and sunshine through the day, with light transient mists and fogs, and occasional passing showers in the afternoon, and early part of the evening, succeeded by clear and serene nights. The winds are at this time somewhat variable; but are most frequently easterly, veering round to the westward in the evening. As the month advances, the weather gradually assumes the more steady and characteristic type of the cold season.

The Hills, in October, are clothed with verdure amid which the variegated flowers of the *Curcuma*, and the waving yellow blossoms of the *Crotularia*, hold in succession the most prominent place. These in their turn give place to the *Gnidia eriocephala*, which continues in flower during the remainder of the cold season. The scenery, too, is rendered peculiarly attractive by the mingled lights and shadows of the mists, which at times flit fitfully across the mountain, now rest in low patches on the vallies, and anon girdle the sides of the mountain ridges with their silvery vapour.

This is the most advantageous period for the invalid to repair to the Hills, when circumstances admit of a choice. It is essentially requisite, however, to have fires in the bungalow for some days previously to its being occupied, in order that all the apartments may be thoroughly dried and ventilated.

During the months of November, December, January, and February, the sky is almost uniformly clear, and the atmosphere dry, cold, bracing, and elastic, with a steady and limited range of temperature. The atmospheric currents are singularly uniform in their direction, force, and duration. During the night and morning, a sharp, steady, easterly wind usually prevails, which, towards mid-day, gradually abates in strength, and veers round to the northward, whence a light breeze continues to blow during the remainder of the day. In the latter part of January, there is a gradual approach to the alternation of land and sea breezes, which become more regular and decided in February, and impart an agreeable softness and mildness to the atmosphere. There is a pretty constant deposition of dew in the early part of the season, in states of the weather favourable to its formation. Occasionally in still, clear nights, the cold is sufficiently great to freeze the dew as it is condensed; and on such occasions hoar frost will be observed, on the fibres of short grass, in the vallies.

Occasional changes of weather are of course to be expected in the course of the season; and they usually occur about the period of the new or full moon. These changes generally consist either in the occurrence of a close and sultry state of the atmosphere, continuing for two or three days, with calm or light southerly airs, accompanied occasionally with distant thunder. and perhaps with one or two showers of rain; or there is an increase in the force of the East wind, which sometimes blows with considerable strength for two or three successive nights, or, more rarely, throughout the twenty-four hours. Although the easterly winds on such occasions are keen and somewhat piercing, the cold is never rigorous.

The clemency of the weather, indeed, even in the coldest months, is one of the most remarkable features of the climate. It is a fact, for which I am unable to find a satisfactory explanation, that at places upwards of two thousand feet lower than this station, and at a distance of not more than twenty or thirty miles, the thermometer occasionally sustains a greater depression by several degrees, than has ever been observed here. Fires are not absolutely required during the day, but are indispensably necessary for comfort in the evenings throughout the cold season.

The atmosphere during these months is generally clear and transparent. Hence the adjacent mountains appear much nearer to the observer, and their features more distinct, than at any other time; and ships sailing near the Coast (and occasionally boats) can frequently be distinguished with the naked eye. In October and November, (and again in the latter months of the hot season), a dense horizontal stratum of mist is often at day-light spread out over the Concan, which it completely shrouds with its fleecy mantle, until dissipated by the beams of the rising sun, when the peaks of the hills are observed, gradually to emerge from under their vapoury covering, like islets from the ocean. These mists are usually seen on such nights as are favourable to the deposition of dew; but what that modification of atmosphere is, which (in the absence of any considerable body of water) at one time, and in one locality, gives rise to the formation of mist, and at another to the deposition of dew, meteorology does not yet enable us fully to explain.

The mean temperature of the cold season is 64° 08′, with a mean daily variation of 11° 72′; the mean maximum heat being 69° 95′ while the mean minimum is 58° 22′. The mean temperature of the season differs only 2° 29′ from the annual mean of the station, and its mean diurnal range is 2° 38′, higher than that of the whole year. The difference of mean temperature between the coldest and hottest months of the season is 2° 64′. The average quantity of rain is 9. 05′ inches—about two-thirds of which fall in October. The average number of days on which rain falls in the season is thirteen.

It will be inferred, from the facts and observations which have now been stated, that the weather, throughout the five months of the cold season, preserves that degree of temperature which is most congenial to the feelings, and which invites to exercise in the open air at all hours; and it is accordingly found, that, on a great proportion of days, persons are able to walk, and ride on horseback, during the greater part of the day, with great comfort, and perhaps without any immediate bad effect. But experience shows (and reasoning teaches us the same lesson) that this luxury, so rarely available in the Tropic Zone, must even here be indulged in by the invalid with exceeding great caution. The causes of this important restriction will be brought under review hereafter.

March ushers in the hot season, the duration of which is extended through the two subsequent months. The atmosphere now assumes a dim and hazy appearance, so that the low-land hills of the Concan, appear distant and indistinct, and the sea is scarcely ever visible, except, perhaps, for an hour or two before sunset, when it may be occasionally seen on that part of the horizon immediately below the sun's disc.

There is a greater and more sudden transition of temperature in March, than occurs in any other month; but the heat, which never attains a great elevation, is very materially tempered and moderated by the cool, soft, and refreshing sea breezes, which prevail with great, and almost unvarying regularity, during these months. They blow at first from N. N. W. but become more westerly, commence at an earlier hour, and increase in strength, as the season advances. They generally, however, set in about 10 o'clock, gradually freshen after noon, and subside in the evening, when, after a short calm, a north-easterly wind springs up and continues during the night to be again succeeded by the sea breeze of the following day. Occasionally, at the commencement of the hot season, the north-easterly wind subsides early in the morning, and there is an interval of one or two hours' duration, during which the atmosphere is still and sultry until the approach of the sea breeze.

The heat is scarcely ever felt to be oppressive within doors; and is certainly much less so than what is experienced during the summer months at the Cape of Good Hope. Solar radiation, however, is very intense, especially during March and April; and consequently exposure to the direct influence of the noon-day sun is both unpleasant to the feelings, and prejudicial to the health. The nights are never close or hot, but are invariably cool and refreshing.

The air attains its greatest degree of heat in April, and of dryness in March. In April, an increase of humidity is perceptible, both by the sensations and by the indications of the moistened thermometer; and towards the end of the month, and in the early part of May, the sky is frequently chequered with clouds, and there are occasional short, but heavy, thunder-showers, usually occurring at one of the principal lunations, which serve to reduce and equalize the temperature. During the latter half of May, the sky is generally clear or partially clouded during the day; but towards sun-set thin mists and fogs begin to rise from the westward horizon, and in a few minutes envelope the hills in their vapoury mantle; and are frequently observed to course rapidly over the mountain when a very light air prevails in the lower strata of the atmosphere. This is succeeded either by a clear, calm, serene night, with low patches of fog resting over some of the vallies, until dissipated by the morning sun; or, if the sea breeze keeps up, partial mists continue to flit over the hills at intervals through the night. This alternate succession of cloud and sunshine, of fogs and mists, along with the more uninterrupted westerly winds which now prevail, contributes very greatly to the coolness and equability of the climate, and renders it, next to October, the most agreeable part of the year.

The superiority of the climate over that of the low country during the hot months, is not more striking than is the contrast between the beauty and variety of foliage, and blossom which now decorate the mountain, and the arid and parched up surface of the plains below.

The mean temperature of the hot season is 72°58,' and the mean daily range is 13° 19,' the mean maximum of temperature being 79° 18,' and its mean minimum 65° 99.' The mean temperature of the season exceeds the annual mean by 6° 21,' and the mean daily variation is 3° 35' higher than that for the year. The difference between the mean temperature of the coldest and the hottest months of the season is only 2° 25.' The mean amount of rain is 2. 84 inches of which the greatest portion falls towards the end of

April and in May. The average number of days on which rain falls is 13.

Although frequent showers of rain usually fall from the beginning of June, the rainy season, strictly speaking, cannot be said to commence till from the 10th to the 15th of the month. Until that date, the weather resembles very much what has been described in characterizing the early part of October. There is the same pleasant variety of sunshine and cloud during the early part of the day, with a more settled westerly wind. Early in the afternoon, as the temperature of the atmosphere begins to decline, and its capacity of dissolving vapor, in consequence, diminishes, watery fogs begin to drift over the table-land, and are not dispersed until two or three hours after sun-rise on the following morning. These fogs gradually augment in density and humidity, and set in earlier, and disperse later, as the month advances.

The commencement of the monsoon is usually preceded by at least one thunder squall, which gives various warnings of its approach. In the early and middle part of the day, the air is found to be still and sultry. Dense, dark, lowering clouds gradually begin to gather in the South East; the general stillness is now broken by the occasional muttering of distant thunder, and, by strong and sudden gusts of wind from the same quarter of the horizon, the masses of clouds rapidly thicken as they advance, and at length, let fall their surcharged moisture in a heavy torrent of rain amid the most beautiful and vivid lightning, and amid peals of thunder which reverberate from mountain to mountain, with a grand and terrific effect.

This is followed, on the succeeding morning, by a clear and transparent sky, and by that delicious freshness of the atmosphere which so invariably follows a fall of rain on these hills.

The wind now fixes steadily in the S. W. or W. S. W., whence it blows with moderate strength; the fogs and mists rapidly thicken, and close in the view on every side; and at length (usually at some time between the 10th and the 15th) the monsoon sets in with a thick drizzling rain, which continues with few interruptions during the remainder of the month.

The hills, during July and August, are enveloped in almost perpetual clouds and fog. The visual horizon is thus limited within a very small circumference; except when at intervals the fog partially opens so as to permit a hasty glimpse of some of the nearer objects, when it again closes in, and shrouds the surface with the same dense gloom as before. The atmosphere is supersaturated with moisture which is precipitated with very little interruption in the form of small, thick, drizzling rain, varying, at short and frequent intervals, with heavy drenching showers, which are often accompanied with a high boisterous wind. The sun's rays, seldom for more than half an hour, or an hour at a time, penetrate the dense mass of cloud with which the sky is shrouded; but at the same time very little cooling takes place by terrestrial radiation, and consequently the climate is rendered not only very equable, but also very temperate. In September, the violence of the monsoon begins to subside. The wind abates in strength, the fogs are much less dense and frequent, and the rainfalls are reduced both in quantity and duration; and towards the latter part of the month there are frequent intervals of clear, fine weather.

The mean temperature of the rainy season is 64° 57′, which corresponds almost exactly with that of the cold season; but the mean daily variation of the former is only 3° 47′, the mean maximum temperature being 66° 31′, and its mean minimum 62° 38′. The mean temperature for the season is 1° 80′ lower than the annual mean; and the mean daily variation is 5° 87′ less than that for the year. The difference between the mean temperature of the coldest and hottest month of the season, is 3° 53′. The average fall of rain is 227.91 inches, of which nearly one-third falls in August. The number of days on which rain falls is 108; there being 14 fair days, of which only two happen in the two months of July and August. The greatest quantity falls in August.

The continuousness of the rain, even more than its total amount, renders the station uninhabitable with comfort during the monsoon, though this season of the year is remarkable for its healthiness. This is to be attributed to the uniformity and temperateness of the climate.

Such is a brief and condensed sketch of the usual progress of the seasons at this station. Their course has been remarkably uniform in the different successive years. The principal deviation, and the one which most affects both the actual temperature and the sensations, consists in the more or less clouded state of the sky in May, and the relative quantity of rain which falls in that month.

The causes of its physical qualities.

The causes upon which its physical qualities depend, may be thus briefly stated:—

1st. The first and most influential of these causes, is the local elevation of the station. The atmosphere, having escaped from about one-sixth of the incumbent pressure, thus becomes rarefied to a considerable extent; its capacity for heat is increased in a corresponding ratio, and its local temperature proportionately reduced. By this altitude of 4500 feet above the level of the sea, it acquires a reduction of climate amounting nearly to 14° below the adjacent plain, which is equivalent to a change of latitude of about 18°. The same cause, there is reason to believe, produces another effect of a less favorable nature—an increased intensity of solar radiation.

2nd. The proximity of the station to the Indian ocean forms an important modifying agent in the constitution of the climate, and gives it, in some degree, an insular character. To this cause we are indebted for the regularity and strength of the sea breezes, which so materially moderate the temperature of the hot season, and impart an agreeable softness and humidity to the atmosphere, which would otherwise be very unpleasantly dry during these months. The remarkable equability of the climate is also to be traced principally to the same source. The vicinity of the sea must obviously give this climate a superiority over that of more inland mountains of equal elevation.

To a combination of the two causes which have now been named—proximity to the sea, and that particular altitude at which the air, from its rarefaction, and reduction of temperature, has its capacity for dissolving vapour, so much reduced as to precipitate part of its aqueous vapour—is to be ascribed the redundant humidity which prevails in the rainy season.

3rd. The small lateral extent of the tableland, by insulating it from the surrounding country, lessens the amount of radiant heat which would be emitted from a more extended plain ; while the diversified nature of the surface gives a certain degree of obliquity to the sun's rays, and thus, in conjunction with the former cause, diminishes somewhat their calorific influence.

4th. Another point to be mentioned, which is connected with the preceding one, is the position of the station on the westerly, or sea-ward brow of a steep and precipitous mountain, the base of which is very little higher than the level of the sea. By this topographical disposition the sea breezes are wafted to it, without being heated by travelling over any intermediate space of equal elevation with the hill itself; and a certain degree of protection is also afforded against the East winds. This position of the station on the verge of the mountain might be open to objection, were the country at its base the seat of endemic fever. This, however, is not the case.

5th. The last cause to be noticed, is the absence of higher ranges in the immediate vicinity, which might have the effect of rendering it liable to sudden and extensive vicissitudes of temperature.

Nothing, in my opinion, would tend more to improve the agreeable qualities of this climate, and, at the same time, prove more conducive to its healthiness, than the diffusion of an additional quantity of aqueous vapour in the atmosphere during the latter months of the cold, and early part of the hot, season. Should the contemplated plan be carried into effect, of forming a lake in the valley of the Yenna, (which appears as if scooped out by the hand of nature for the purpose), by throwing a dam cross its narrow outlet, it will not only prove a great ornament to the station, but go a considerable way towards remedying the inconvenience now complained of. To this plan there may be brought forward, as an objection, the danger of malaria, and its attendant diseases. There is not, however, much ground for such an apprehension. We have already seen that, even during the south-west monsoon, when 227 inches of rain fall in little more than three months, the ground never assumes a muddy or swampy appearance; and diseases of malarious origin at this station have never come under my observation.

Its influence on physique.

We now proceed to examine the influence of the climate upon the respiratory function of the lungs. We have seen that the atmosphere of this station is rarefied to the extent of diminishing its pressure upon the system to about one-sixth of its total amount. It is evident, that at each ordinary inspiration a person takes in one-sixth less air than he would do at the level of the sea. Hence a necessity arises either for a greater dilatation of the air-cells of the lungs, or for an increase in the number of respirations. To this is to be added the increased impetus given to the pulmonary circulation by the diminished barometrical pressure, and a consequent augmentation of the quantity of blood to be aerated. No inconvenience, however, is ever experienced here, even on first arrival, in a healthy condition of the respiratory organs; the lungs being enabled, by an increase of action, to meet this additional demand made upon them. Running, or rapid walking, up an acclivity, may perhaps produce breathlessness sooner, or to a greater degree, than similar exercise would on the plains; but the "tightness in the chest and oppression of breathing," complained of on first ascending the Neilgherries, is never felt here, so far as I am aware of. But it follows, from what has been stated, that the climate will be injurious in cases of disease, where the respiration is already limited either by obstruction of any of the bronchial tubes or air-cells, or by other pulmonary lesion. It is important, however, to remark, in connection with this subject that inflammatory affections of the lungs, or Pleura, are of extremely rare occurrence, either among Europeans or Natives, at this station.

The last subject of enquiry, and the one to which the preceding observations are subservient, is the investigation of the sanative influence of the climate; or, in other words, of the uses to which it may be applied as an auxiliary remedy in the treatment of disease. If the view which has been given of its physiological effects be founded upon correct observation—if its mode of operation be essentially tonic and stimulant, and its action be exerted upon the general system, it will follow that the same principles which guide us in the administration of tonic medicines will direct us in the application of this climate to particular diseases.

The efficacy of change of climate in the treatment of disease has been recognized in all countries and in all ages. Without being able to explain the rationale of its agency, it is nevertheless a fact familiar to every medical man, and particularly so to every practitioner in India, that many diseases, which resist every other remedy, are frequently alleviated or removed by change of climate, or sometimes even by change of air. It is not to be expected, however, that climate alone will cure the disease. It ought only to be considered as an auxiliary remedy, placing the patient on a position where the system is more tolerant of other necessary remedies, and where the disease is more amenable to the action of medicine. Hence medical treatment and dietetic regimen, with certain modifications, are equally necessary, (and are sometimes even more imperatively required), in the one locality as in the other.

It my be useful briefly to advert to certain precautions necessary to be observed by the invalid on his arrival at this station. We have seen that there will be at first a tendency to repletion from the increased action of the sanguiferous vessels, acting on a system already excited by travelling, and from the increased activity of the digestive functions. To counteract any bad effects which might result from these causes, it will be necessary to avoid all extraneous sources of stimulation; to abstain for a short time from too much muscular exertion; to avoid exposure to the noon-day sun; to pay due attention to the state of the bowels; and to keep a curb upon the appetite (if inordinately increased) by a sparing use of stimulant articles of diet, and by lessening for a short time the customary allowance of wine, or other fermented liquors. It will require very little argument to demonstrate the utility of restriction in regard to diet. The invalid will soon learn, from personal experience, that the appetite outstrips the digestion, and that over-indulgence in the pleasures of the table will be followed by its usual dyspeptic accompaniments. This, however, is the least of the injurious consequences to be apprehended: an evil of greater magnitude is, that, by supplying a greater quantity of nutriment than the system has previously been accustomed to, another cause of stimulation is added to the excitement already produced by the diminished atmospheric pressure. This caution it behoves every invalid carefully to bear in mind; and where there is any tendency to visceral plethora, whether inflammatory or congestive, it becomes of paramount importance.

After the system has recovered from the excitement of travelling, and from the first re-action of the climate, the valetudinarian ought to be, as much as possible, in the open air during the mornings and afternoons, keeping within doors during the heat of the day. He ought also to avoid exposing himself at an early hour in the morning to the high easterly winds which occasionally blow during the cold weather, and prove injurious to the delicate invalid, especially if suffering from recurrences of fever. It is much better that such patients should be deprived of exercise for a few mornings than that they should run the risk of suffering a relapse of fever, to which these high east winds powerfully contribute. The kind and degree of exercise must be adapted to the strength of the patient, and to the nature of his disease. Speaking generally, exercise on horseback will at first be more beneficial than walking. It is less fatiguing and it has a less accelerating effect upon the pulse and respiration; while, at the same time, it promotes in a greater degree the abdominal circulation. The more healthy and robust may profitably combine both. But whatever kind of exercise may be had recourse to, it ought never to be carried to the extent of producing fatigue. If the invalid experiences much lassitude, or if, on the contrary, he feels heated and excited in the evening, the inference may be drawn in both cases that the exercise has been carried beyond the capabilities of the system.

Warm clothing is so obviously indicated, that it may be considered superfluous to adduce any arguments in its support. It is important, however, to enjoin strict attention to this point in the case of children, who, from their generating less heat than adults, have their temperature more easily lowered.*

---

* This paper was presented by Dr. James Murray, Superintendent of the Convalescent Station at Mahabaleshwar, to the Medical and Physical Society of Bombay on the 31st November 1836, and was published in the first volume of its Transactions. From this paper only a few important extracts are given above.

APPENDIX II.

SHORT NOTES ON THE PRESENT ALTERED CLIMATE OF MAHABLESHWAR AND ITS CAUSES.

(BY Mr. J. C. LISBOA.)

The able medical officers who have acted as superintendents of the station since its establishment in 1828, have from time to time given to the public full particulars of the climate, topography, etc., of the place. It is therefore not my intention to refer to these subjects and I will at once proceed to the subject of this paper.

Old residents and visitors who saw this place 20 years ago are unanimously of opinion that it has been growing warmer year by year—a belief confirmed by the thermometrical readings noted by Drs. Murray and McConaghy. From Dr. Murray's observations extending from 1829-36 it is seen that the mean temperature of the hot season was 72° 19′ with a mean daily variation of 13° 19′. The mean maximum being 79° 18′ and the mean minimum 65° 99′. The mean temperature of the cold season was 64° 08′ and the mean daily range 11° 72; the mean maximum 69° 95′ while the mean minimum was 58° 22′. The mean of the rainfall of the 8 years was 239·80 inches. From Dr. McConaghy's observations from 1874 to 1880 it is calculated that the mean temperature of the hot season is 80°3 with a mean daily range of 25°88′—the mean maximum being 86°81′ and minimum 60°93′. The mean temperature of the cold season is 69°91′ the mean maximum 74°6′ and the mean minimum 54°30′ with a mean daily variation of 19°76′. The mean rainfall of the seven years is 238·49 inches.* I may here say that no readings have been given for 1881, as they were not to be had at the time these notes were taken, but such private observations as were recorded by me lead me to think that in 1881 the temperature kept much the same as in the preceding years, if it did not rise a little.

What are the causes that have operated to bring about this change? So far as I can judge, since Dr. Murray wrote some 45 years ago, new roads have been opened, old ones widened and many new houses built, the compounds of almost all of which have been denuded of trees to a greater or less extent, and the majority of roofs covered with corrugated iron. Old Points have been enlarged, and two or three new ones I believe added necessitating the cutting down of trees. In some places the trees and shrubs have been trimmed and cleared away to obtain a better view of the scenery and secure a free circulation of air. If the new roads be shaded by large trees as some of the old ones are, and the eastern part of the top of the hill wooded, the climate of Mahableshwar will I think be much improved as there is no doubt that the climate of all tropical

* In these calculations I have followed Dr. Murray who divides the seasons thus :—Cold, comprising October, November, December, January and February; and hot, embracing March, April and May.

countries is cooled down by vegetation. A writer says:—"It has been shown that a tree is a living "creature working for its daily food; it expends force "in its vital processes. But this expenditure requires "an absorption of energy in the form of heat which is "converted into work, and as the only heat available "for the tree is solar heat, it follows that the whole "work done by the trees is at the expense of such "heat either direct or from the earth. This is no "inconsiderable matter when the whole internal work "of a tree is considered and this is multiplied by "thousands. This specific heat of a living tree is "about 56° Fahr; it maintains this heat in cold and "in hot weather—hence large masses of trees must "appreciably cool a climate which is ordinarily "above 56°. The evaporation from the leaf surface "is enormous. Trees of no unusual size may have "several thousand leaves representing several acres "of surface and each leaf is covered with mouths "which incessantly exhale moisture. Evaporation "is attended by an absorption of heat, that is by "coolness; this is the principle of the freezing "machines in daily use; hence another item in the "cooling power of trees. To this must be added the "vast reflecting and radiating power of the leaf "surfaces which throw into the air the heat that "would otherwise be absorbed into the earth. It is "known that stones absorb heat above all other "natural surfaces; hence the intense heat of a stony "surface. A screen of trees consequently protects "such a surface from the excessive absorption and "consequent radiation of heat."

As will have been observed, there is no perceptible difference in the rainfall of the last few years as compared with that registered some 44 years ago; and yet the complaint is that the water supply in the wells, tanks and springs of Mahableshwar is diminishing from year to year chiefly in May, The explanation of this is to be sought for in the fact above mentioned that the large forest trees attract the vapour-laden clouds and convert them into rain in much the same way as before, but the latter, not meeting the surface-obstacles to the same extent as formerly, rushes to the rivers, and part of the rain-water which ought to have sunk to the deeper strata of the earth and to the rills from which the wells, tanks, and springs receive their regular and steady supply, is rapidly evaporated, because in consequence of the thick brushwood being cut and thinned there is exposed to the rays of the tropical sun a large stony surface which cannot be sufficiently protected by the shade of the thin screen of the large trees.

But the interesting question whether large trees being planted close to the banks of nullahs and wells the supply of water is diminished is not yet settled. Dr. Cook, who was Superintendent of Mahableshwar, says "the opportunity of making a practical ex-"periment on the subject was afforded me last "year, the result of which has convinced me that "great loss is experienced in dry climates by allow-"ing large trees to grow in immediate contiguity "to water-courses. While engaged in excavating a "tank for the supply of water to Malcolm Peth, I "observed one of the supply streams to be gradually "failing until in dry weather it had dwindled "altogether away and the nullah had become dry; "I then caused the trees which grew thickly on the "sides of the ravines to be cut down for a distance "of thirty or forty yards, and others further up to "be thinned and cleared. Within a few days water "again appeared in the nullah, and in a short time "commenced to flow as before.'' If this be confirmed by experiments conducted by equally competent persons in various parts of the country, ghauts and plains, and under varying circumstances, then there would be no objection to the thinning of the trees for a few yards around the tanks and lakes, as is I believe already done in some parts of the hill. But such experiments should be made with great caution for the facts as observed at Matheran by Dr. Smith are not very encouraging. The stream in the Bund valley which when covered by a jungle of trees and reeds was full of water has become since these were cleared, tiny in the hot season.

Notwithstanding this increase of temperature the station is the healthiest we have in this Presidency and its climate invigorating particularly to such as have been debilitated by the heat of the plains or hard-work. In November, December and January, Europeans and natives find a fire in the hearth very desirable. The hot season embraces the months of March, April and May. The hottest month of the year is April when the temperature rises occasionally very high, the dry easterly winds blowing from the Deccan being very trying; but the mornings and evenings are always cool and make outdoor exercise pleasant. From about the 20th of the month the temperature begins to fall gradually down to the end of May, the north-westerly moist sea-breezes which now prevail with more or less regularity serving to moderate the heat and make the season agreeable.

Cases of malarious fevers are scarcely or never met with, except those which are sent from below. We occasionally see poor natives with distended abdomens due to enlarged spleens and livers; these generally come from the marshy districts and low lying localities of Nagotna, etc., and even these cases are more amenable to treatment and susceptible of improvement after a few months' residence on the hill. Coughs and colds are also rare at Mahableshwar, as variations of temperature are not so great here as on the plains. On that account too the climate is particularly beneficial to persons suffering from wasting diseases of the lungs, especially incipient phthisis, and to those tainted with hereditary tubercular or scrofulous diatheses.

Mahableshwar is also said to be suited to cases of uterine disorders, and also diseases of children and infants.

For invalids and visitors there are several "Points" and places of amusement, commanding magnificent views of the plains below; also Badminton courts and Lawn tennis grounds; a good library, "Frere Hall," situated in a convenient locality, a large lake with fruit and flower gardens on its banks affording recreation to many who resort to it every evening. When H. E. the Governor is at the station, he kindly allows his band to play twice or thrice a week at some of the Points.

Flower gardens, in the compounds of bungalows, which served for the recreation of visitors, chiefly invalids, are now getting rare. Roses and fuschias, &c., thrive well.

Now as to the way of ascertaining the height and temperature of a given place without the use of an instrument.

The habits of animals and plants carefully studied will serve us as a guide nearly as sure as the instruments at present used for ascertaining the temperature and height of a given place; for there is for each species of animal and plant life a fixed range of heat and height beyond which it cannot live. In the examination of individual cases other considerations, such as composition of the soil, its capacity for absorbing and retaining moisture, etc., must be also taken into consideration. There are at present very few facts available, but few as they are, they might serve to illustrate my statement.

None of the species by which the Orders *Anonaceæ* and *Guttiferæ* are abundantly represented in the Concan, Malabar, and other low countries,—plants which love heat and moisture and are sensitive of cold are as yet discovered on the top of Mahableshwar. The following species belonging to these two orders are seen at Matheran :—

Uvaria Narum, *Bocagea Dalzellii* (*Sageri*) *Garcinia Indica* (*Kokam*), *G. ovalifolia* (*Tawir*), *Ochrocarpus longifolius* (*Surüngi*). None of them, nor *Coculus macrocarpus* (*wat wail*) *Mäcaranga Indica* (*Chanda*) and many others very common at that hill have as yet been described from Mahableshwar. The height to which *Uvaria Narum* ascends is 4,000 feet above the level of the sea; *Garcinia ovalifolia* 3,000 ft., *Cassia fistula* 4,000 and *Bridelia retusa* 3,500 feet. These plants ascend as high as the valleys of Mahableshwar —the upper extremity of their range and no more. *Terminalia chebula* (*Hirda*) which ascends 5,000 feet is very common on the top of this hill, but its congener *T. Bellerica* (*Berdà*) grows common only along the foot of the ghauts. Again there are numerous plants at Matheran which are common to it and to the surrounding districts of the Concan, and a few restricted to that station and to the higher ghauts but none peculiar or confined to the hill.

The Flora of Mahableshwar consists chiefly of plants seen in the plains and lower ghauts but in addition there are found a few species which are not described as yet from any other place in this presidency; they are *Turræa villosa*, *Lysimachia obovata*, *Swertia decussata*, *Micromeria Malcolmiana*, *Piper Hookerü*, *Dabregeasia longifolia*, *Curcuma caulina*, *Crynum brachynemum*, *and Usnea vulgatissima*. If these species are not met with on the lower ranges, which are thoroughly explored, it is because the heat of the plains and lower ghauts and perhaps other circumstances are not favourable to their existence there.

The upper range of the several plants mentioned above have been taken from observations made in various hills in Madras, Bengal and elsewhere

where they have been found growing. Now, if under identical circumstances of soil and climate you find on ascending a hill a plant, say *Garcinia ovalifolia* growing till you have reached a certain height and then no more, while beyond and above, you meet till a certain further height, say *Uvaria Narum* or *Cassia fistula*, you will take it that in the first instance you were at about 3,000 feet and in the latter about 4,000 feet above the level of the sea. And if you find *Terminalia chebula* (above referred to) growing in full vigour beyond, your calculation of the altitude receives further confirmation from this fact.

Bridelia retusa ascends as high as 3,500 feet:—hence it is not found growing at the Station; but appears on the slopes below the Bombay Point.

The distribution of animal life is subject to the same laws. Animals, birds and insects which make their appearance in great numbers at Matheran in the hot season are not seen on the top of Mahableshwar. We particularly miss here "our cousins" the monkeys which at Matheran come and go often in herds crashing through the woods and climbing up the trees chiefly the *Chanda* (*Macaranga India*) which at that season are full of round fleshy capsules of the size of a pea, crack these with great noise, voraciously pushing down their pouches the kernels, chattering and grinning, "their way of talking and laughing" specially when a stouter member of the fraternity falls down carrying with him the slender branch on which he was resting, while at the foot of the trees there sits an old *patriarch* watching the feasting of the younger members some of whom will now and then join him and comb his gray hairs with their nails. After taking their repast they all go back as they come to distant places whence their booming cry can often be heard.*

No one who has visited Matheran during the hot season will ever forget the strong stridulous noise of a small black insect about 2 inches long named *Cicada ducalis.* "In the middle of the day "its screeching is at its height, and when resting "on a tree close by the noise is deafening. It "lasts some time too, and it is a matter of wonder "to notice with how little apparent effort a sound "so intense and penetrating is produced." (Dr. Smith on Matheran). This sound ceases at night and in the mornings, and the insect apparently disappears, when the cool breezes set in towards the middle of May. This disagreeable shrill is occasionally heard at Mahableshwar in the hotter part of the summer.

The same process is with due alteration applicable to the determination of temperature of a given locality.

My knowledge of botany is very limited and of Zoology still more so; I will therefore dwell no further on the habits of plants and animals, but conclude with short notes on the useful plants

---

* A gentleman who has been to Mahableshwar regularly for the last five years states that he only once saw monkeys coming from a valley up to "Lodwick Point," one of the lowest points of the station.

mentioned above and a few others found generally on the hill, hoping they will prove of interest to you.

Swertia decussata—(Kaddu or Kandi-bitter) is a gentian about 2 feet high densely leafy, and bearing numerous white flowers. It is sold in the bazaar at Mahableshwar in a dried state in bundles containing about 20 to 30 plants. It differs from *Ophelia chireta* officinal in the Indian Pharmacopœa by its stem being winged while that of the latter is round, and from *Andrographis paniculata* which is named *Kreat* and also used in this country as a bitter, from the stem of the latter, though quadrangular, not being winged. The stems are used in infusion as a bitter tonic for correcting the defective functions of the stomach. How came the hill people, ignorant as they are, to the knowledge of the effects of this drug employing it for the cure of the same complaints as gentian is used in Europe and elsewhere? Did instinct lead them to its use? Probably so.

We have an instance very analogous. Dr. Cornish after stating that during the late famine in Madras, thousands of people lived on the leaves of *Erythroxylon monogynum,* remarks that it is the instinct that must have led the Indian famine stricken people to have recourse to the leaves of this shrub in preference to many others which grew in its neighbourhood. *E. monogynum* is a congener of the Coca (*E. coca*) which is used by the Americans chiefly when they have to make long journeys carrying with them as little food as possible. It is a powerful stimulant, hard physical exertion and long endurance of hunger being possible under its use. The effects are due to the alkaloid *cocaina* and are analogous to those of opium. The following is another instance: "*Caladium Seguinum,* W. or Dum Cane of America is used in the West Indies and South America to set sugar; and two years ago the writer failing to bring some (Imphee?) syrup to a good grain, found that the native sugar makers of Poona use the stalk of the three species of Caladium here catalogued for the purpose. The natives of Bombay could not have learnt this from the West Indies, and such remarkable coincidences of which Bombay offers many instances, deserve the attention of philologists." (Birdwood—*Vegetable Productions, p.p. 144.*).

Micromeria Malcolmiana (*Piprimut*) was first noticed by Mr. Law of the Bombay C. S., one of the earliest investigators of Indian Botany, and subsequently minutely described by Mr. Dalzell. This learned botanist says that it is entitled to be called Indian peppermint; in its aromatic and carminative properties it rivals the peppermint of Europe.

It is a small herbaceous plant about 1½ to 2 feet high with slender branches, distant leaves about 8 to 9 lines long and small blue coloured flowers, arranged in umbellate cymes. Grows wild on both the banks of the Yenna river. It is not seen on the top of the station, it appears therefore that it cannot thrive on ground above 4,000 feet.

I do not know that this plant has been described from any other presidency nor whether it is ever utilized. It is hoped that the authorities, the Revenue Commissioner and the Collector, who have been doing their utmost to forward the interests of this district will try to induce the hill men and especially the owners of large gardens to cultivate it and extract its oil.

Actinodaphne Hookeri (*Pisa*).—The commonest tree after Jambul. The under surface of the leaves is glaucous. The infusion is reckoned a powerful diuretic and is used in chronic inflammation of the uterus, bladder and urethra and in the irritability left after the cure of gonorrhœa.

Randia dumetorum (*Ghella*).—Very common. The fruit is used to intoxicate fish as well as an emetic.

Lasiosiphon eriocephalus (*Rametta*) is a shrub or small tree very common at Mahableshwar and at Matheran; it is often seen stripped of its bark which is employed to intoxicate fish, (and thus catch it) in ponds and tanks. This practice of catching fish, killing indiscriminately even the small ones which are not fit for eating is general throughout India. For this purpose numerous plants are used such as Kakmari, Tivas, Nivol, Atki, &c., the latter is very common at Mahableshwar.

Trichosantes palmata (*Koundal*).—Stem angular, very long, running over the highest trees, covered with gray scabrous somewhat corky bark; the young green parts smooth. The fruit is reckoned poisonous. The natives pound it and mix it with cocoanut oil to make an appplication for indolent sores. It is also used by them in ozœna. Inhalation of the smoke of the burnt roots of this plant has been employed in cynanche tonsillaris. The orange red fruit is used for decorating the canopy over the temporary altar raised in Hindu houses on the occasion of the Dasara festival.

Evodia Roxburghiana.—The dry seeds are slightly aromatic and are used as a stomachic along with some bitter.

Salix tetrasperma (*Wallung, bacha*).—This ornamental tree is very common at Mahableshwar and is at once recognised by the beautiful white colour of the undersurface of the leaves. Dalzell and Gibson say that the bark is used as a febrifuge, a fact which my own observations have confirmed. It is worth a trial; perhaps it may be as efficacious as the salicylic acid extracted from the exotic species. From both (exotic and indigenous) a very fine charcoal is obtained; it has been tried as a base for gunpowder, which is more free from various neutral salts than is that made from other charcoal, but on this account the strength of the powder is inferior, though considerably superior as regards long preservation without deterioration of quality.

Curcuma canlina (*Chowar*) mentioned above is a plant confined to Mahableshwar; it belongs to the ginger tribe and is very abundant during the rains everywhere specially on the table land. Taken to Bombay it flowered in September. From its large bulb arrowroot was formerly manufactured by the Chinese and by one Mr. da Costa and sold to the Commissariat and in the Bombay bazaars. It is stated by Dr. McConaghy that in 1878 from 500 to 600 lbs. were prepared by a European resident and samples sent to Messrs. Kemp and Treacher for their opinion. "The colour and taste were pronounced good but it was found deficient in nutritive properties." I believe praiseworthy offorts are still being made by the Sattara Collector and the Commissioner of the Central Division to have this arrowroot well prepared and its quality again thoroughly tested. According to Royxburgh, Royle and Birdwood arrowroot known as *tickar* arrowroot is manufactured in many parts of India from the bulbs of *Curcuma angustifolia*, *C. montana*, and other bulbs common in this presidency and elsewhere. That which is sold in the English market as *East India arrowroot* or *Travancore arrowroot* is, it is believed, exported from S. India prepared from *Maranta Arundinacea*, with which is often mixed some portion of *tickar* arrowroot.*

---

* This paper was read by Dr. J. C. Lisboa, before the Grant Medical College Society, Bombay, in 1881, and published in its Transactions.

APPENDIX III.

HEREDITARY MANAGERS OF PRATAPGAD AND MAHABLESHWAR.

The Pingles.

Moro Trimal Pingle, the Prime Minister of Shivaji, the founder of the Maratha Empire, built the Fort of Pratapgad and the Temple of Mahableshwar in 1656. In recognition of his valuable services Shivaji appointed him the manager of both the places, and granted him a sanad to continue the management perpetually in his family. In accordance with the letter and spirit of the sanad, the management of the temples at both the places have been to this day continued to the family of this renowned Minister of Shivaji. The Pingles are called Mujumdars at Pratapgad and Vahiwatdars at Mahableshwar. Their hereditary connection with these historical places, their high descent, and the part they played in the history of the Marathas, support a claim for their mention in this book.

The ancestors of the Pingle family are said to be known to fame as having held high and important offices under the Mahomedan governments of Bijapur and Golconda. The first person, who was selected by Shahaji Bhosle in 1636, to be the manager of the country held by him in the Carnatic, on account of his administrative talents and integrity, was Trimalacharya, a Deshastha Brahmin, from whom authentic history of the Pingles can be traced. Trimalacharya first accompanied Shahaji to Tanjore from Nasik in the Deccan. Shivaji, the son of Shahaji, bestowed the office of Primer Minister on Moropant Pingle, the son of Trimalacharya, in 1659. Moropant held the post for a period of thirty two years, and distinguished himself by personal valour and extraordinary talents. Captain Grant Duff, the historian of the Marathas, has borne ample testimony to the character and merits of this personage. The selection of Moropant Pingle by Shivaji to the highest office in the kingdom is a sufficient guarantee of his superior fitness. He helped Shivaji in establishing and maintaining a vast empire. He was a gallant soldier and sagacious statesman. He won several battles and acquired large territory for his master. His ability, prudence and bravery made such an impression on Shivaji, that when he went to Delhi in 1666, he vested full authority of his kingdom in Moropant Pingle and two others, and enjoined all persons to respect and obey his orders as if issued by himself. The services of such a faithful and devoted minister cannot be too highly spoken of. After the death of Shivaji at Raygad in 1680, his son Sambhaji succeeded to the throne. He imprisoned Moropant Pingle along with other ministers of Shivaji, but soon released the former, who died in 1681. Later on, Sambhaji nominated Nilo Moreshwar, the eldest son of Moropant, as the chief manager of the affairs of government in the Carnatic, administered for many years by his grandfather, Trimalacharya. After nine years of the civil administration in the Carnatic (about 1692), during the reign of Rajaram, second son of Shivaji, Nilopant succeeded his father in the office of the Peshwa or Prime Minister. He enjoyed the dignity and honour of this office for eighteen years. Rajaram, in one of his sanads, conferring an Inam of Rs. 20,000 on Nilopant, signified his appreciation of the services of the Pingles in the following terms:—"You are the ancient and hereditary servant of our Empire, and your family has on many a difficult occasion made great sacrifices for the sake of our Empire. These eminent services of yours render it very necessary and imperative for the State to support your distinguished family forever." Nilopant, who adhered to Tarabai, died at Rangna, shortly after the accession of Raja Shahu to the Satara throne.

In 1687, Kesopant Pingle, the brother of the late Peshwa, Nilopant, was appointed to command an expedition into the Carnatic; while Yeshwant Rao Pingle exercised supreme control over the garrisons maintained on the various forts of the Maratha Empire.

In 1712, Queen Tarabai, wife of Rajaram, founded the Kolhapur principality and enthroned her son Sambhaji at Panhala. She was pleased to bestow the office and dignity of Peshwa upon Kesopant Pingle, who had made himself sufficiently famous in the Carnatic campaign of 1687. He administered the State efficiently for some years as Peshwa; and his son, Bhagvant Rao, and grandson Bhavan Rao, successively held the Peshwaship of the Kolhapur dynasty for a considerable time.

In 1708, Raja Shahu, the son of Sambhaji, returned from the Mogal Camp to Satara, and installed himself on the throne as the rightful heir of the elder branch of Shivaji's family. He conferred the Peshwaship on Bahiropant Pingle, the second son of Moropant, the first Minister of Shivaji. While in the exercise of this office and in the full enjoyment of his soverign's favour and confidence, he was deputed in 1713 to repel Kanhoji Angria, the then powerful Chief of Kolaba in the Konkan, who, taking advantage of the dissensions in the Satara family, refused to owe allegiance to the paramount power, and was making efforts to establish an independent state for himself. Bahiropant was unfortunately defeated in this expedition against the Angria, and for that simple reason, incurred great displeasure of Raja Shahu, who removed him from the office of the Peshwa and appointed in his place, Balaji Vishwanath Bhat, a Chitpavan Brahmin, then in the service of Dhanaji Jadhav, as Peshwa. He afterwards rose to great distinction. His descendants usurped the authority of the Satara kings for themselves and established their capital at Poona.

Owing to this unhappy incident and the instability of the Prince's favour, the office of Peshwa, which the Pingles enjoyed for fifty-eight years, ceased to exist in their family in 1716, and with it, as a consequence, they lost all power and importance they possessed for several generations, in different parts of the Maratha Empire. The descendants of the first family in the Empire were thus soon reduced to insignificance, if not to obliterate the very name of Pingle from the annals of their country. The kind-hearted Raja Shahu, however, on being requested to consider the valuable services rendered to his ancestors by the Pingles, was pleased to grant certain districts and forts, including Pratapgad, to this family in perpetuity, which yielded an annual income sufficient to maintain its honour and dignity. After the death of Raja Shahu, the succeeding Rajas of Satara became mere puppets in the hands of the Peshwas of Poona; and the Pingle family fell an easy prey to the rapacity of the Peshwas, who resumed under some pretext or other, even the handsome grant given by Raja Shahu, which was said to yield Rs 60,000 a year. Even this small income forming the residue of their Jahagir, with the fort of Pratapgad and Mahableshwar, was resumed by the Peshwa, Madhavrao I, in 1768, who granted, in lieu, an annual income of ten thousand Rupees to Naropant, Madhav Rao and Raghunath Rao, the then representatives of the Pingle family, in the following manner:—

Rs. 1,000 Inam.
Rs. 5,000 Personal Saranjam.
Rs. 4,000 Cash allowance.

This grant too was continued only upto the accession of Baji Rao II to the Peshwaship in 1796, who attached it under the plea of levying a cess of "Saranjam Puttee." His real aim and object was to resume small Jahagirs and estates throughout the country. Thus, the only means of subsistence of the Pingle family being taken away, they were reduced to a most pitiable condition. Through the intervention of Dowlat Rao Sindia, Bajirao II eventually issued orders for the relinquishment of the holdings of Madhav Rao Pingle, but unfortunately he was waylaid and murdered by one of the gangs of the notorious free-booters led by Chattersing, and consequently the family was thrown in a helpless condition.

On the overthrow of the Peshwa's rule at Poona, in 1818 the British Government was established in the Deccan. The advent of the British was then considered a happy omen that revived the drooping spirit of several influencial and old Maratha families scattered over the Empire, who had suffered greatly under the oppressive and unrighteous administration of the last Peshwa, Bajirao II. The Hon'ble Mr. Mountstuart Elphinstone, who made settlement in the Deccan, enlisted the sympathies of the public by helping the fallen and depressed families. The representative of the Pingle family was then one Bahiropant, a boy of 10 years only. The Hon'ble Mr. Elphinstone on full enquiry found that "the family of Moropant Pingle, the 1st Peshwa, were in a state of great destitution and have nothing for their maintenance," and generously granted to it an allowance of Rs. 1,800 per annum from the Poona Treasury. H. H. Chhatrapati Pratapsingh, the Raja of Satara, who was raised to the Satara throne in 1818 by the British Government, was also pleased to recognise the claims of the Pingle family by bestowing an allowance of Rs. 480 per annum on Bahiropant. This political stipend was continued to Bahiropant by H. H. Chhatrapati Shahaji alias Appasaheb Maharaj, the last Raja of Satara. On the demise of that Prince in 1848, it was further continued by the British Government on the recommendation of the Commissioner, Mr. (afterwards Sir) Bartle Frere, till the death of Bahiropant in 1856. The present surviving member of the senior branch of the Pingle family is Pandurang Dattatraya Pingle, grandson of Bahiropant. He is a third class Sardar of the Deccan and chief manager of the Pratapgad and Mahableshwar temples. For managing these temples he gets a remuneration of Rs. 400 (Rs. 300 for Pratapgad and Rs. 100 for Mahableshwar). There are also other members of the Pingle family enjoying Inam lands at Wathar in the Satara District.

GENEALOGY OF THE PINGLE FAMILY.

- Trimalacharya.
  - Moropant.
    - Nilopant.
    - Bahiropant.
      - Apajipant.
        - Naropant.
          - Bahiropant.
            - Dattopant
              - Pandurang Rao.
            - Anand Rao.
            - Moropant.
            - Krishna Rao.
    - Yeshwant Rao.
      - Govind Rao.
        - Naropant.
          - Dhondopant.
            - Raghunath Rao.
              - Narayan Rao.
          - Madhao Rao.
  - Kesopant.

APPENDIX IV.

IRON SMELTING AT MAHABALESHWAR.

Captain George Le Grand Jacob (afterwards General Sir Le Grand Jacob), in a paper read before the Bombay Branch of the Royal Asiatic Society in 1839, gives the following account of Iron Smelting at Mahabaleshwar:—

"This is described as being conducted in primeval simplicity and rudeness. The ore is dug from a depth of from twenty to thirty feet, and has the appearance of a course gravel. Before being submitted to the furnace, it is pounded, and freed from dust. The furnace is an oval excavation in the earth, on which is fitted a cover of baked clay. The excavation is lined with charcoal powder, over which is placed a layer of small charcoal; and in the centre of this bed is placed a clay pipe uniting the nozzles of two goat-skin bellows. When thus prepared, the top of the furnace is fastened over the excavation, and stopped all round with clay. Charcoal is then poured into a hole in the top, which acts as a chimney. It requires three hours to smelt twelve seers of ore, producing a lump of iron weighing about 5½ seers. This lump undergoes a hammering on an anvil, to free it from dross, which considerably reduces its weight, and which is still further reduced in the processes of manufacturing it up into articles for use; so that the ore is found to contain not more than thirty per cent. of iron. This, although sold in the bazars at less than a penny per pound, was undersold by a superior quality of English iron, which found its way to the same markets."*

---

* Captain Le Grand Jacob read also another paper before the Bombay Branch of the Royal Asiatic Society:—" Note on the alleged periodical rise of a sacred river at Mahabaleshwar," in which he says:—" This is a juggle of Brahminical priests, who pretend that, in addition to the five rivers, which they say take their rise from the mouth of Mahadeva's sacred bull, at Mahabaleshwar, a sixth makes its appearance every twelfth year. At this auspicious time, numbers flock to wash away their sins, and fee the Brahmins who administer to their credulity. The priests taking care that the cheat shall not be discovered by prohibiting all access to the temple whence the water is said to issue."

APPENDIX V.

CHINESE CONVICTS.

"About three years after the station was started a Jail was established for Chinese and Malay convicts, as it was found that the climate of Poona and Thana was injurious to their health. The Jail, which was constructed to contain about 120 prisoners, is thus described by Dr. Winchester in 1857:—"The Jail is built in a quadrangular form with an inner paved court. The front, or entrance side, contains rooms for the guard of sepoys, offices for the Jail authorities, and two rooms used as solitary cells, or as places for prisoners when too sick to walk to hospital or requiring quiet and separate attendance. The other three sides of the Jail are composed of long, lofty and very airy apartments, entered only from the inner quadrangle. Two of these sides were generally occupied by the prisoners, while the third was used as a store and workroom." The Jail stood on the ground at present occupied by the P. W. D. Bungalow. From the reports of different Superintendents, it appears that the prisoners, though convicted of such grave crimes as murder, piracy, and robbery, were quiet and amenable to discipline. Each convict received a daily ration of 1½ annas. During working hours, from 8 A.M. to 4 P.M., they were required to work for Government. With few exceptions they were shut up at six in the evening, though lights were allowed till 8 or 9 o'clock; and during this time the majority of the prisoners occupied themselves in different kinds of indoor work. During their leisure hours, they were allowed to visit the Bazar and get provisions. A number availed themselves of this liberty to plant potatoes and other English vegetables in the adjoining fields, which could be easily irrigated, and they were allowed to enjoy the profit derived from their sale. A few convicts of good character were occasionally allowed the privilege of working all day in their potato-fields and of sleeping in them during the night, on condition that substitutes were provided for the Government work. The privilege was seldom abused. The principal labour in which the prisoners were employed was the construction of station roads. They were also frequently employed in preparing arrow-root for the Commissariat Department; as much as 3,500 pounds were supplied in one cold season. The Chinese greatly improved the station gardens; and it is owing, in great measure, to their industry, that potatoes and English vegetables have been so great a success. They also taught the inhabitants to make cane baskets and chairs. When the Jail was abolished in 1864, the majority of prisoners obtained tickets of leave, and some of these were permitted to remain on the hill, on condition of presenting themselves on the 1st of every month at the Superintendent's office. Misconduct rendered them liable to forfeit their liberty and be sent to the Poona Jail. Now there are no Chinamen on the hill, and their gardens have gone to the hands of the Malis, Kunbis and Dhavads."*

---

* *Mahabaleshwar Guide*, p. 45, 46 (1897).

APPENDIX VI.

LIST OF EARLY VISITORS TO MAHABALESHWAR.

The following is the list of the early visitors to Mahabaleshwar who subscribed to the Road Fund, started in 1829 at Malcolm Peith :—

Sir John Malcolm.
W. Newnham.
Sir C. Malcolm.
Lady Malcolm.
Mrs. Stewart.
Miss Stewart.
Dr. Walker.
P. W. LeGeyt.
Captain Nutt.
Ensign Auld.
G. Malcolm.
J. Graham.
J. Murray.
Captain Graham.
Captain Malcolm.
C. Soins.
M. Dickenson.
Lieut.-Col. Robertson.
Major Barnewell.
C. Norris.
J. Bird.
G. L. Elliot.
A. Grafton.
J. C. Hawkins.
Lieut. Brown.
Lieut. Horn.
L. R. Reid.
A. Turner.
James Wright.
D. B. Smith.
Lieut. Foster.
Ensign Russell.
R. D. Luard.
J. Luard.
Rev. J. Payne.
Sir Sidney Beckwith.
Major Powell.
Captain Wilson.
Captain Fawcett.
A. Hammond.
R. Robertson.
J. Crow.
G. C. Tawrin.
Mrs. Tawrin.
Captain Jameson.
" P. D. Otley.
M. Dunlop.
W. Malet.

K. A. Jackson.
Capt. Freemantle.
Mr. Carless.
Lieut.-Col. Hardy.
E. Frederick.
Captain Manson.
P. M. Melwill
W. Money.
J. Swanson.
Captain Bonomy.
Catain Nusyes.
J. Dickenson.
H. Fawcett.
J. K. O. Williams.
W. Lester.
H. Holland.
C. Wells.
J. Henderson.
G. Giberne.
H. J. Robertson.
M. Wish.
G. Grant.
J. Molesworth.
H. P. Hadow.
Mrs. Hadow.
Lieut. Candy.
Mrs. Cogan.
Mrs. Gibart.
H. Wyndham.
Major Stock.
Lieut. R. Lambert.
Captain Lighton.
J. H. Wilson.
W. Johnson.
Captain Boyd.
H. Lumsden.
Lieut. Jacob.
J. Little.
T. B. Hamilton.
H. Havelock.
D. Blane.
Sir Keith Jackson.
C. Hunter.
W. Haughton.
E. Wilson.
J. Bax.
A. Bell.
A. Morse.
R. Foster.
C. Giberne.
B. Rooke.
H. Reeves.
Randall Ward.
J. Jopp.
T. M. Turner.
Lieut.-Col. Lodwick.
Col. Thomas.
J. Stevens.
Captain Simpson.
Sir J. W. Awdry.
Lieut.-Col. Russell.
D. Scott.
E. C. Jones.
J. Warden.
Mrs. Willoughby.
Mrs. Dickenson.
Sir J. Barnes,
&c., &c.

APPENDIX VII.

STATEMENT SHOWING THE RAINFALL AT MAHABALESHWAR FROM THE YEAR 1829 TO 1915.

[From the records of the Mahabaleshwar Civil Hospital.]

Year.	Rainfall.		Year.	Rainfall.	
	Inches.	Cents.		Inches.	Cents.
1829	257	...	1847	278	...
1830	232	...	1848	245	...
1831	185	...	1849	347	...
1832	226	...	1850	285	...
1833	302	...	1851	255	...
1834	297	...	1852	345	...
1835	226	...	1853	318	...
1836	243	...	1854	222	...
1837	267	...	1855	228	...
1838	180	...	1856	251	...
1839	233	...	1857	252	...
1840	284	...	1858	245	...
1841	281	...	1859	210	..
1842	304	...	1860	248	...
1843	285	...	1861	316	78
1844	262	...	1862	243	85
1845	249	...	1863	281	33
1846	288	...	1864	261	15

Year.	Rainfall.		Year.	Rainfall.	
	Inches.	Cents.		Inches.	Cents.
1865	265	88	1891	260	85
1866	280	...	1892	270	71
1867	215	43	1893	285	81
1868	235	61	1894	310	65
1869	175	85	1895	246	76
1870	260	39	1896	402	41
1871	203	...	1897	267	24
1872	268	86	1898	296	66
1873	271	8	1899	139	60
1874	298	40	1900	333	78
1875	340	13	1901	260	28
1876	243	18	1902	224	22
1877	167	63	1903	269	48
1878	255	42	1904	234	43
1879	278	18	1905	199	29
1880	207	74	1906	217	86
1881	261	13	1907	297	69
1882	374	49	1908	311	2
1883	296	90	1909	277	29
1884	329	48	1910	246	74
1885	272	68	1911	202	76
1886	263	16	1912	265	51
1887	292	30	1913	226	62
1888	278	90	1914	332	4
1889	255	98	1915	230	96
1890	322	67			